FREE Study Skills Videos/I

Dear Customer,

Thank you for your purchase from Mometrix! We consider it an honor and a privilege that you have purchased our product and we want to ensure your satisfaction.

As part of our ongoing effort to meet the needs of test takers, we have developed a set of Study Skills Videos that we would like to give you for FREE. These videos cover our *best practices* for getting ready for your exam, from how to use our study materials to how to best prepare for the day of the test.

All that we ask is that you email us with feedback that would describe your experience so far with our product. Good, bad, or indifferent, we want to know what you think!

To get your FREE Study Skills Videos, you can use the **QR code** below, or send us an **email** at studyvideos@mometrix.com with *FREE VIDEOS* in the subject line and the following information in the body of the email:

- The name of the product you purchased.
- Your product rating on a scale of 1-5, with 5 being the highest rating.
- Your feedback. It can be long, short, or anything in between. We just want to know your impressions and experience so far with our product. (Good feedback might include how our study material met your needs and ways we might be able to make it even better. You could highlight features that you found helpful or features that you think we should add.)

If you have any questions or concerns, please don't hesitate to contact me directly.

Thanks again!

Sincerely,

Jay Willis
Vice President
jay.willis@mometrix.com
1-800-673-8175

SIE

Exam Prep 2022-2023

3 Full-Length Practice Tests

Secrets Study Guide Book for the FINRA Securities Industry Essentials

3rd Edition

Written and edited by the Mometrix Financial Industry Certification Test Team

Printed in the United States of America

This paper meets the requirements of ANSI/NISO Z39.48-1992 (Permanence of Paper).

ISBN 13: 978-1-5167-2164-1
ISBN 10: 1-5167-2164-0

DEAR FUTURE EXAM SUCCESS STORY

First of all, **THANK YOU** for purchasing Mometrix study materials!

Second, congratulations! You are one of the few determined test-takers who are committed to doing whatever it takes to excel on your exam. **You have come to the right place.** We developed these study materials with one goal in mind: to deliver you the information you need in a format that's concise and easy to use.

In addition to optimizing your guide for the content of the test, we've outlined our recommended steps for breaking down the preparation process into small, attainable goals so you can make sure you stay on track.

We've also analyzed the entire test-taking process, identifying the most common pitfalls and showing how you can overcome them and be ready for any curveball the test throws you.

Standardized testing is one of the biggest obstacles on your road to success, which only increases the importance of doing well in the high-pressure, high-stakes environment of test day. Your results on this test could have a significant impact on your future, and this guide provides the information and practical advice to help you achieve your full potential on test day.

Your success is our success

We would love to hear from you! If you would like to share the story of your exam success or if you have any questions or comments in regard to our products, please contact us at **800-673-8175** or **support@mometrix.com**.

Thanks again for your business and we wish you continued success!

Sincerely,
The Mometrix Test Preparation Team

TABLE OF CONTENTS

Introduction

Thank you for purchasing this resource! You have made the choice to prepare yourself for a test that could have a huge impact on your future, and this guide is designed to help you be fully ready for test day. Obviously, it's important to have a solid understanding of the test material, but you also need to be prepared for the unique environment and stressors of the test, so that you can perform to the best of your abilities.

For this purpose, the first section that appears in this guide is the **Secret Keys**. We've devoted countless hours to meticulously researching what works and what doesn't, and we've boiled down our findings to the five most impactful steps you can take to improve your performance on the test. We start at the beginning with study planning and move through the preparation process, all the way to the testing strategies that will help you get the most out of what you know when you're finally sitting in front of the test.

We recommend that you start preparing for your test as far in advance as possible. However, if you've bought this guide as a last-minute study resource and only have a few days before your test, we recommend that you skip over the first two Secret Keys since they address a long-term study plan.

If you struggle with **test anxiety**, we strongly encourage you to check out our recommendations for how you can overcome it. Test anxiety is a formidable foe, but it can be beaten, and we want to make sure you have the tools you need to defeat it.

Secret Key #1 – Plan Big, Study Small

There's a lot riding on your performance. If you want to ace this test, you're going to need to keep your skills sharp and the material fresh in your mind. You need a plan that lets you review everything you need to know while still fitting in your schedule. We'll break this strategy down into three categories.

Information Organization

Start with the information you already have: the official test outline. From this, you can make a complete list of all the concepts you need to cover before the test. Organize these concepts into groups that can be studied together, and create a list of any related vocabulary you need to learn so you can brush up on any difficult terms. You'll want to keep this vocabulary list handy once you actually start studying since you may need to add to it along the way.

Time Management

Once you have your set of study concepts, decide how to spread them out over the time you have left before the test. Break your study plan into small, clear goals so you have a manageable task for each day and know exactly what you're doing. Then just focus on one small step at a time. When you manage your time this way, you don't need to spend hours at a time studying. Studying a small block of content for a short period each day helps you retain information better and avoid stressing over how much you have left to do. You can relax knowing that you have a plan to cover everything in time. In order for this strategy to be effective though, you have to start studying early and stick to your schedule. Avoid the exhaustion and futility that comes from last-minute cramming!

Study Environment

The environment you study in has a big impact on your learning. Studying in a coffee shop, while probably more enjoyable, is not likely to be as fruitful as studying in a quiet room. It's important to keep distractions to a minimum. You're only planning to study for a short block of time, so make the most of it. Don't pause to check your phone or get up to find a snack. It's also important to **avoid multitasking**. Research has consistently shown that multitasking will make your studying dramatically less effective. Your study area should also be comfortable and well-lit so you don't have the distraction of straining your eyes or sitting on an uncomfortable chair.

The time of day you study is also important. You want to be rested and alert. Don't wait until just before bedtime. Study when you'll be most likely to comprehend and remember. Even better, if you know what time of day your test will be, set that time aside for study. That way your brain will be used to working on that subject at that specific time and you'll have a better chance of recalling information.

Finally, it can be helpful to team up with others who are studying for the same test. Your actual studying should be done in as isolated an environment as possible, but the work of organizing the information and setting up the study plan can be divided up. In between study sessions, you can discuss with your teammates the concepts that you're all studying and quiz each other on the details. Just be sure that your teammates are as serious about the test as you are. If you find that your study time is being replaced with social time, you might need to find a new team.

Secret Key #2 – Make Your Studying Count

You're devoting a lot of time and effort to preparing for this test, so you want to be absolutely certain it will pay off. This means doing more than just reading the content and hoping you can remember it on test day. It's important to make every minute of study count. There are two main areas you can focus on to make your studying count.

Retention

It doesn't matter how much time you study if you can't remember the material. You need to make sure you are retaining the concepts. To check your retention of the information you're learning, try recalling it at later times with minimal prompting. Try carrying around flashcards and glance at one or two from time to time or ask a friend who's also studying for the test to quiz you.

To enhance your retention, look for ways to put the information into practice so that you can apply it rather than simply recalling it. If you're using the information in practical ways, it will be much easier to remember. Similarly, it helps to solidify a concept in your mind if you're not only reading it to yourself but also explaining it to someone else. Ask a friend to let you teach them about a concept you're a little shaky on (or speak aloud to an imaginary audience if necessary). As you try to summarize, define, give examples, and answer your friend's questions, you'll understand the concepts better and they will stay with you longer. Finally, step back for a big picture view and ask yourself how each piece of information fits with the whole subject. When you link the different concepts together and see them working together as a whole, it's easier to remember the individual components.

Finally, practice showing your work on any multi-step problems, even if you're just studying. Writing out each step you take to solve a problem will help solidify the process in your mind, and you'll be more likely to remember it during the test.

Modality

Modality simply refers to the means or method by which you study. Choosing a study modality that fits your own individual learning style is crucial. No two people learn best in exactly the same way, so it's important to know your strengths and use them to your advantage.

For example, if you learn best by visualization, focus on visualizing a concept in your mind and draw an image or a diagram. Try color-coding your notes, illustrating them, or creating symbols that will trigger your mind to recall a learned concept. If you learn best by hearing or discussing information, find a study partner who learns the same way or read aloud to yourself. Think about how to put the information in your own words. Imagine that you are giving a lecture on the topic and record yourself so you can listen to it later.

For any learning style, flashcards can be helpful. Organize the information so you can take advantage of spare moments to review. Underline key words or phrases. Use different colors for different categories. Mnemonic devices (such as creating a short list in which every item starts with the same letter) can also help with retention. Find what works best for you and use it to store the information in your mind most effectively and easily.

Secret Key #3 – Practice the Right Way

Your success on test day depends not only on how many hours you put into preparing, but also on whether you prepared the right way. It's good to check along the way to see if your studying is paying off. One of the most effective ways to do this is by taking practice tests to evaluate your progress. Practice tests are useful because they show exactly where you need to improve. Every time you take a practice test, pay special attention to these three groups of questions:

- The questions you got wrong
- The questions you had to guess on, even if you guessed right
- The questions you found difficult or slow to work through

This will show you exactly what your weak areas are, and where you need to devote more study time. Ask yourself why each of these questions gave you trouble. Was it because you didn't understand the material? Was it because you didn't remember the vocabulary? Do you need more repetitions on this type of question to build speed and confidence? Dig into those questions and figure out how you can strengthen your weak areas as you go back to review the material.

Additionally, many practice tests have a section explaining the answer choices. It can be tempting to read the explanation and think that you now have a good understanding of the concept. However, an explanation likely only covers part of the question's broader context. Even if the explanation makes perfect sense, **go back and investigate** every concept related to the question until you're positive you have a thorough understanding.

As you go along, keep in mind that the practice test is just that: practice. Memorizing these questions and answers will not be very helpful on the actual test because it is unlikely to have any of the same exact questions. If you only know the right answers to the sample questions, you won't be prepared for the real thing. **Study the concepts** until you understand them fully, and then you'll be able to answer any question that shows up on the test.

It's important to wait on the practice tests until you're ready. If you take a test on your first day of study, you may be overwhelmed by the amount of material covered and how much you need to learn. Work up to it gradually.

On test day, you'll need to be prepared for answering questions, managing your time, and using the test-taking strategies you've learned. It's a lot to balance, like a mental marathon that will have a big impact on your future. Like training for a marathon, you'll need to start slowly and work your way up. When test day arrives, you'll be ready.

Start with the strategies you've read in the first two Secret Keys—plan your course and study in the way that works best for you. If you have time, consider using multiple study resources to get different approaches to the same concepts. It can be helpful to see difficult concepts from more than one angle. Then find a good source for practice tests. Many times, the test website will suggest potential study resources or provide sample tests.

Practice Test Strategy

If you're able to find at least three practice tests, we recommend this strategy:

Untimed and Open-Book Practice

Take the first test with no time constraints and with your notes and study guide handy. Take your time and focus on applying the strategies you've learned.

Timed and Open-Book Practice

Take the second practice test open-book as well, but set a timer and practice pacing yourself to finish in time.

Timed and Closed-Book Practice

Take any other practice tests as if it were test day. Set a timer and put away your study materials. Sit at a table or desk in a quiet room, imagine yourself at the testing center, and answer questions as quickly and accurately as possible.

Keep repeating timed and closed-book tests on a regular basis until you run out of practice tests or it's time for the actual test. Your mind will be ready for the schedule and stress of test day, and you'll be able to focus on recalling the material you've learned.

Secret Key #4 – Pace Yourself

Once you're fully prepared for the material on the test, your biggest challenge on test day will be managing your time. Just knowing that the clock is ticking can make you panic even if you have plenty of time left. Work on pacing yourself so you can build confidence against the time constraints of the exam. Pacing is a difficult skill to master, especially in a high-pressure environment, so **practice is vital**.

Set time expectations for your pace based on how much time is available. For example, if a section has 60 questions and the time limit is 30 minutes, you know you have to average 30 seconds or less per question in order to answer them all. Although 30 seconds is the hard limit, set 25 seconds per question as your goal, so you reserve extra time to spend on harder questions. When you budget extra time for the harder questions, you no longer have any reason to stress when those questions take longer to answer.

Don't let this time expectation distract you from working through the test at a calm, steady pace, but keep it in mind so you don't spend too much time on any one question. Recognize that taking extra time on one question you don't understand may keep you from answering two that you do understand later in the test. If your time limit for a question is up and you're still not sure of the answer, mark it and move on, and come back to it later if the time and the test format allow. If the testing format doesn't allow you to return to earlier questions, just make an educated guess; then put it out of your mind and move on.

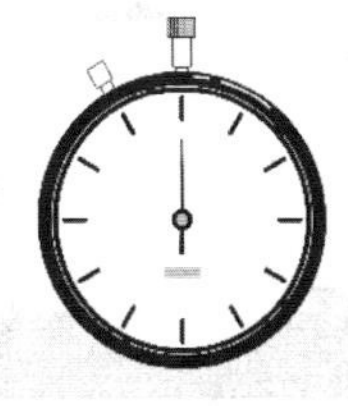

On the easier questions, be careful not to rush. It may seem wise to hurry through them so you have more time for the challenging ones, but it's not worth missing one if you know the concept and just didn't take the time to read the question fully. Work efficiently but make sure you understand the question and have looked at all of the answer choices, since more than one may seem right at first.

Even if you're paying attention to the time, you may find yourself a little behind at some point. You should speed up to get back on track, but do so wisely. Don't panic; just take a few seconds less on each question until you're caught up. Don't guess without thinking, but do look through the answer choices and eliminate any you know are wrong. If you can get down to two choices, it is often worthwhile to guess from those. Once you've chosen an answer, move on and don't dwell on any that you skipped or had to hurry through. If a question was taking too long, chances are it was one of the harder ones, so you weren't as likely to get it right anyway.

On the other hand, if you find yourself getting ahead of schedule, it may be beneficial to slow down a little. The more quickly you work, the more likely you are to make a careless mistake that will affect your score. You've budgeted time for each question, so don't be afraid to spend that time. Practice an efficient but careful pace to get the most out of the time you have.

Secret Key #5 – Have a Plan for Guessing

When you're taking the test, you may find yourself stuck on a question. Some of the answer choices seem better than others, but you don't see the one answer choice that is obviously correct. What do you do?

The scenario described above is very common, yet most test takers have not effectively prepared for it. Developing and practicing a plan for guessing may be one of the single most effective uses of your time as you get ready for the exam.

In developing your plan for guessing, there are three questions to address:

- When should you start the guessing process?
- How should you narrow down the choices?
- Which answer should you choose?

When to Start the Guessing Process

Unless your plan for guessing is to select C every time (which, despite its merits, is not what we recommend), you need to leave yourself enough time to apply your answer elimination strategies. Since you have a limited amount of time for each question, that means that if you're going to give yourself the best shot at guessing correctly, you have to decide quickly whether or not you will guess.

Of course, the best-case scenario is that you don't have to guess at all, so first, see if you can answer the question based on your knowledge of the subject and basic reasoning skills. Focus on the key words in the question and try to jog your memory of related topics. Give yourself a chance to bring the knowledge to mind, but once you realize that you don't have (or you can't access) the knowledge you need to answer the question, it's time to start the guessing process.

It's almost always better to start the guessing process too early than too late. It only takes a few seconds to remember something and answer the question from knowledge. Carefully eliminating wrong answer choices takes longer. Plus, going through the process of eliminating answer choices can actually help jog your memory.

Summary: Start the guessing process as soon as you decide that you can't answer the question based on your knowledge.

How to Narrow Down the Choices

The next chapter in this book (**Test-Taking Strategies**) includes a wide range of strategies for how to approach questions and how to look for answer choices to eliminate. You will definitely want to read those carefully, practice them, and figure out which ones work best for you. Here though, we're going to address a mindset rather than a particular strategy.

Your odds of guessing an answer correctly depend on how many options you are choosing from.

Number of options left	5	4	3	2	1
Odds of guessing correctly	20%	25%	33%	50%	100%

You can see from this chart just how valuable it is to be able to eliminate incorrect answers and make an educated guess, but there are two things that many test takers do that cause them to miss out on the benefits of guessing:

- Accidentally eliminating the correct answer
- Selecting an answer based on an impression

We'll look at the first one here, and the second one in the next section.

To avoid accidentally eliminating the correct answer, we recommend a thought exercise called **the $5 challenge**. In this challenge, you only eliminate an answer choice from contention if you are willing to bet $5 on it being wrong. Why $5? Five dollars is a small but not insignificant amount of money. It's an amount you could afford to lose but wouldn't want to throw away. And while losing $5 once might not hurt too much, doing it twenty times will set you back $100. In the same way, each small decision you make—eliminating a choice here, guessing on a question there—won't by itself impact your score very much, but when you put them all together, they can make a big difference. By holding each answer choice elimination decision to a higher standard, you can reduce the risk of accidentally eliminating the correct answer.

The $5 challenge can also be applied in a positive sense: If you are willing to bet $5 that an answer choice *is* correct, go ahead and mark it as correct.

Summary: Only eliminate an answer choice if you are willing to bet $5 that it is wrong.

Which Answer to Choose

You're taking the test. You've run into a hard question and decided you'll have to guess. You've eliminated all the answer choices you're willing to bet $5 on. Now you have to pick an answer. Why do we even need to talk about this? Why can't you just pick whichever one you feel like when the time comes?

The answer to these questions is that if you don't come into the test with a plan, you'll rely on your impression to select an answer choice, and if you do that, you risk falling into a trap. The test writers know that everyone who takes their test will be guessing on some of the questions, so they intentionally write wrong answer choices to seem plausible. You still have to pick an answer though, and if the wrong answer choices are designed to look right, how can you ever be sure that you're not falling for their trap? The best solution we've found to this dilemma is to take the decision out of your hands entirely. Here is the process we recommend:

Once you've eliminated any choices that you are confident (willing to bet $5) are wrong, select the first remaining choice as your answer.

Whether you choose to select the first remaining choice, the second, or the last, the important thing is that you use some preselected standard. Using this approach guarantees that you will not be enticed into selecting an answer choice that looks right, because you are not basing your decision on how the answer choices look.

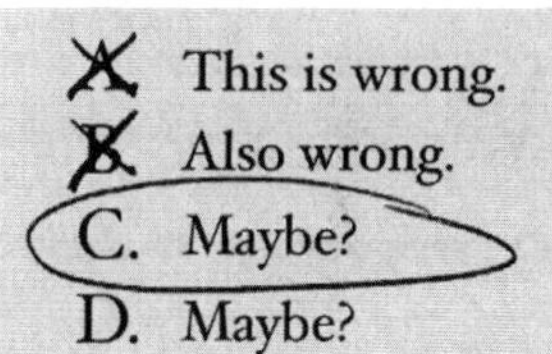

This is not meant to make you question your knowledge. Instead, it is to help you recognize the difference between your knowledge and your impressions. There's a huge difference between thinking an answer is right because of what you know, and thinking an answer is right because it looks or sounds like it should be right.

Summary: To ensure that your selection is appropriately random, make a predetermined selection from among all answer choices you have not eliminated.

Test-Taking Strategies

This section contains a list of test-taking strategies that you may find helpful as you work through the test. By taking what you know and applying logical thought, you can maximize your chances of answering any question correctly!

It is very important to realize that every question is different and every person is different: no single strategy will work on every question, and no single strategy will work for every person. That's why we've included all of them here, so you can try them out and determine which ones work best for different types of questions and which ones work best for you.

Question Strategies

✅ Read Carefully

Read the question and the answer choices carefully. Don't miss the question because you misread the terms. You have plenty of time to read each question thoroughly and make sure you understand what is being asked. Yet a happy medium must be attained, so don't waste too much time. You must read carefully and efficiently.

✅ Contextual Clues

Look for contextual clues. If the question includes a word you are not familiar with, look at the immediate context for some indication of what the word might mean. Contextual clues can often give you all the information you need to decipher the meaning of an unfamiliar word. Even if you can't determine the meaning, you may be able to narrow down the possibilities enough to make a solid guess at the answer to the question.

✅ Prefixes

If you're having trouble with a word in the question or answer choices, try dissecting it. Take advantage of every clue that the word might include. Prefixes can be a huge help. Usually, they allow you to determine a basic meaning. *Pre-* means before, *post-* means after, *pro-* is positive, *de-* is negative. From prefixes, you can get an idea of the general meaning of the word and try to put it into context.

✅ Hedge Words

Watch out for critical hedge words, such as *likely, may, can, sometimes, often, almost, mostly, usually, generally, rarely,* and *sometimes.* Question writers insert these hedge phrases to cover every possibility. Often an answer choice will be wrong simply because it leaves no room for exception. Be on guard for answer choices that have definitive words such as *exactly* and *always.*

✅ Switchback Words

Stay alert for *switchbacks.* These are the words and phrases frequently used to alert you to shifts in thought. The most common switchback words are *but, although,* and *however.* Others include *nevertheless, on the other hand, even though, while, in spite of, despite,* and *regardless of.* Switchback words are important to catch because they can change the direction of the question or an answer choice.

✓ Face Value

When in doubt, use common sense. Accept the situation in the problem at face value. Don't read too much into it. These problems will not require you to make wild assumptions. If you have to go beyond creativity and warp time or space in order to have an answer choice fit the question, then you should move on and consider the other answer choices. These are normal problems rooted in reality. The applicable relationship or explanation may not be readily apparent, but it is there for you to figure out. Use your common sense to interpret anything that isn't clear.

Answer Choice Strategies

✓ Answer Selection

The most thorough way to pick an answer choice is to identify and eliminate wrong answers until only one is left, then confirm it is the correct answer. Sometimes an answer choice may immediately seem right, but be careful. The test writers will usually put more than one reasonable answer choice on each question, so take a second to read all of them and make sure that the other choices are not equally obvious. As long as you have time left, it is better to read every answer choice than to pick the first one that looks right without checking the others.

✓ Answer Choice Families

An answer choice family consists of two (in rare cases, three) answer choices that are very similar in construction and cannot all be true at the same time. If you see two answer choices that are direct opposites or parallels, one of them is usually the correct answer. For instance, if one answer choice says that quantity *x* increases and another either says that quantity *x* decreases (opposite) or says that quantity *y* increases (parallel), then those answer choices would fall into the same family. An answer choice that doesn't match the construction of the answer choice family is more likely to be incorrect. Most questions will not have answer choice families, but when they do appear, you should be prepared to recognize them.

✓ Eliminate Answers

Eliminate answer choices as soon as you realize they are wrong, but make sure you consider all possibilities. If you are eliminating answer choices and realize that the last one you are left with is also wrong, don't panic. Start over and consider each choice again. There may be something you missed the first time that you will realize on the second pass.

✓ Avoid Fact Traps

Don't be distracted by an answer choice that is factually true but doesn't answer the question. You are looking for the choice that answers the question. Stay focused on what the question is asking for so you don't accidentally pick an answer that is true but incorrect. Always go back to the question and make sure the answer choice you've selected actually answers the question and is not merely a true statement.

✓ Extreme Statements

In general, you should avoid answers that put forth extreme actions as standard practice or proclaim controversial ideas as established fact. An answer choice that states the "process should be used in certain situations, if…" is much more likely to be correct than one that states the "process should be discontinued completely." The first is a calm rational statement and doesn't even make a definitive, uncompromising stance, using a hedge word *if* to provide wiggle room, whereas the second choice is far more extreme.

✓ Benchmark

As you read through the answer choices and you come across one that seems to answer the question well, mentally select that answer choice. This is not your final answer, but it's the one that will help you evaluate the other answer choices. The one that you selected is your benchmark or standard for judging each of the other answer choices. Every other answer choice must be compared to your benchmark. That choice is correct until proven otherwise by another answer choice beating it. If you find a better answer, then that one becomes your new benchmark. Once you've decided that no other choice answers the question as well as your benchmark, you have your final answer.

✓ Predict the Answer

Before you even start looking at the answer choices, it is often best to try to predict the answer. When you come up with the answer on your own, it is easier to avoid distractions and traps because you will know exactly what to look for. The right answer choice is unlikely to be word-for-word what you came up with, but it should be a close match. Even if you are confident that you have the right answer, you should still take the time to read each option before moving on.

General Strategies

✓ Tough Questions

If you are stumped on a problem or it appears too hard or too difficult, don't waste time. Move on! Remember though, if you can quickly check for obviously incorrect answer choices, your chances of guessing correctly are greatly improved. Before you completely give up, at least try to knock out a couple of possible answers. Eliminate what you can and then guess at the remaining answer choices before moving on.

✓ Check Your Work

Since you will probably not know every term listed and the answer to every question, it is important that you get credit for the ones that you do know. Don't miss any questions through careless mistakes. If at all possible, try to take a second to look back over your answer selection and make sure you've selected the correct answer choice and haven't made a costly careless mistake (such as marking an answer choice that you didn't mean to mark). This quick double check should more than pay for itself in caught mistakes for the time it costs.

✓ Pace Yourself

It's easy to be overwhelmed when you're looking at a page full of questions; your mind is confused and full of random thoughts, and the clock is ticking down faster than you would like. Calm down and maintain the pace that you have set for yourself. Especially as you get down to the last few minutes of the test, don't let the small numbers on the clock make you panic. As long as you are on track by monitoring your pace, you are guaranteed to have time for each question.

✓ Don't Rush

It is very easy to make errors when you are in a hurry. Maintaining a fast pace in answering questions is pointless if it makes you miss questions that you would have gotten right otherwise. Test writers like to include distracting information and wrong answers that seem right. Taking a little extra time to avoid careless mistakes can make all the difference in your test score. Find a pace that allows you to be confident in the answers that you select.

⊘ Keep Moving

Panicking will not help you pass the test, so do your best to stay calm and keep moving. Taking deep breaths and going through the answer elimination steps you practiced can help to break through a stress barrier and keep your pace.

Final Notes

The combination of a solid foundation of content knowledge and the confidence that comes from practicing your plan for applying that knowledge is the key to maximizing your performance on test day. As your foundation of content knowledge is built up and strengthened, you'll find that the strategies included in this chapter become more and more effective in helping you quickly sift through the distractions and traps of the test to isolate the correct answer.

Now that you're preparing to move forward into the test content chapters of this book, be sure to keep your goal in mind. As you read, think about how you will be able to apply this information on the test. If you've already seen sample questions for the test and you have an idea of the question format and style, try to come up with questions of your own that you can answer based on what you're reading. This will give you valuable practice applying your knowledge in the same ways you can expect to on test day.

Good luck and good studying!

Three-Week SIE Exam Study Plan

On the next few pages, we've provided an optional study plan to help you use this study guide to its fullest potential over the course of three weeks. If you have six weeks available and want to spread it out more, spend two weeks on each section of the plan.

Below is a quick summary of the subjects covered in each week of the plan.

- Week 1: Knowledge of Capital Markets & Understanding Products and Their Risks
- Week 2: Understanding Trading, Customer Accounts, and Prohibited Activities & Overview of the Regulatory Framework
- Week 3: Practice Tests

Please note that not all subjects will take the same amount of time to work through.

Three full-length practice tests are included in this study guide. We recommend saving the third test and any additional tests for after you've completed the study plan. Take these practice tests without any reference materials a day or two before the real thing as practice runs to get you in the mode of answering questions at a good pace.

Week 1: Knowledge of Capital Markets & Understanding Products and Their Risks

Instructional Content

First, read carefully through the Knowledge of Capital Markets & Understanding Products and Their Risks chapters in this book, checking off your progress as you go:

- ❑ Regulatory Entities, Agencies, and Market Participants
- ❑ Market Structure
- ❑ Economic Factors
- ❑ Offerings
- ❑ Additional Rules and Regulations (Knowledge of Capital Markets)
- ❑ Products
- ❑ Investment Risks
- ❑ Additional Rules and Regulations (Understanding Products and Their Risks)

As you read, do the following:

- Highlight any sections, terms, or concepts you think are important
- Draw an asterisk (*) next to any areas you are struggling with
- Watch the review videos to gain more understanding of a particular topic
- Take notes in your notebook or in the margins of this book

After you've read through everything, go back and review any sections that you highlighted or that you drew an asterisk next to, referencing your notes along the way.

Week 2: Understanding Trading, Customer Accounts, and Prohibited Activities & Overview of the Regulatory Framework

Instructional Content

First, read carefully through the Understanding Trading, Customer Accounts, and Prohibited Activities & Overview of the Regulatory Framework chapters in this book, checking off your progress as you go:

- ❑ Trading, Settlement, and Corporate Actions
- ❑ Customer Accounts and Compliance Considerations
- ❑ Prohibited Activities
- ❑ Additional Rules and Regulations (Understanding Trading, Customer Accounts, and Prohibited Activities)
- ❑ SRO Regulatory Requirements for Associated Persons
- ❑ Employee Conduct and Reportable Events
- ❑ Additional Rules and Regulations (Overview of the Regulatory Framework)

As you read, do the following:

- Highlight any sections, terms, or concepts you think are important
- Draw an asterisk (*) next to any areas you are struggling with
- Watch the review videos to gain more understanding of a particular topic
- Take notes in your notebook or in the margins of this book

After you've read through everything, go back and review any sections that you highlighted or that you drew an asterisk next to, referencing your notes along the way.

Week 3: Practice Tests

Your success on test day depends not only on how many hours you put into preparing, but also on whether you prepared the right way. It's good to check along the way to see if your studying is paying off. One of the most effective ways to do this is by taking practice tests to evaluate your progress. Practice tests are useful because they show exactly where you need to improve. Every time you take a practice test, pay special attention to these three groups of questions:

- The questions you got wrong
- The questions you had to guess on, even if you guessed right
- The questions you found difficult or slow to work through

This will show you exactly what your weak areas are, and where you need to devote more study time. Ask yourself why each of these questions gave you trouble. Was it because you didn't understand the material? Was it because you didn't remember the vocabulary? Do you need more repetitions on this type of question to build speed and confidence? Dig into those questions and figure out how you can strengthen your weak areas as you go back to review the material.

Practice Test #1

Now that you've read over the instructional content, it's time to take a practice test. Complete Practice Test #1. Take this test with **no time constraints**, and feel free to reference the applicable sections of this guide as you go. Once you've finished, check your answers against the provided answer key. For any questions you answered incorrectly, review the answer rationale, and then **go back and review** the applicable sections of the book. The goal in this stage is to understand why you answered the question incorrectly, and make sure that the next time you see a similar question, you will get it right.

Practice Test #2

Next, complete Practice Test #2. This time, give yourself **1 hour and 45 minutes** to complete all of the questions. You should again feel free to reference the guide and your notes, but be mindful of the clock. If you run out of time before you finish all of the questions, mark where you were when time expired, but go ahead and finish taking the practice test. Once you've finished, check your answers against the provided answer key, and as before, review the answer rationale for any that you answered incorrectly and then go back and review the associated instructional content. Your goal is still to increase understanding of the content but also to get used to the time constraints you will face on the test.

As you go along, keep in mind that the practice test is just that: practice. Memorizing these questions and answers will not be very helpful on the actual test because it is unlikely to have any of the same exact questions. If you only know the right answers to the sample questions, you won't be prepared for the real thing. **Study the concepts** until you understand them fully, and then you'll be able to answer any question that shows up on the test.

Knowledge of Capital Markets

Regulatory Entities, Agencies, and Market Participants

Securities and Exchange Commission (SEC)

The High-Level Purpose and Mission of Securities Regulation

Securities laws date back to the early twentieth century following the stock market crash of 1929. The years 1933 and 1934 saw significant regulatory progress. The Securities Act of 1933 focused on transparent financial reporting and fairness in securities sales. The Securities Exchange Act of 1934 established the Securities and Exchange Commission (SEC) and granted the SEC regulatory power, authority, and oversight of the securities markets including issuance, exchanges, broker firms, and other organizations. Securities laws are in place to protect the public from improper behavior or business practices in the securities industry. A few regulations with narrower scopes were issued over the next decade including the Trust Indenture Act in 1939, the Investment Company Act in 1940, and the Investment Advisers Act of 1940. However, the securities industry would not see another substantial change in regulation for another 60 years until the passage of the Sarbanes-Oxley Act (SOX) of 2002 which followed a year of numerous massive accounting frauds. SOX called for management accountability, transparency in disclosures, and truthfulness in financial reporting.

Definition, Jurisdiction, and Authority of the SEC

The **Securities and Exchange Commission (SEC)** is responsible for ensuring that market participants have adequate information with which to make informed investment decisions. Thus, the SEC monitors securities exchanges, brokers and dealers, investment advisers, mutual funds, and other market participants to ensure that they are following the established securities laws. The SEC is responsible for monitoring these market participants within the broad guidelines set forth in securities laws such as the Securities Act of 1933, the Securities Exchange Act of 1934, and the Sarbanes-Oxley Act of 2002. In order to properly enforce these broad provisions, the SEC engages in rulemaking to clarify its role in specific circumstances and provide guidance to public filers. Companies with securities traded on a public exchange must file periodic financial reports with the SEC. The public then has access to these reports through the SEC's database.

The SEC enforces regulations through civil or administrative action, as well as criminal lawsuits. Civil action is appropriate in instances where an individual must return illegally gained profits, while administrative action is more appropriate where the punishment is to be barred from participation in the financial markets, and criminal lawsuits are appropriate for outright financial crimes.

Self-Regulatory Organizations (SROs)

A regulatory organization is an organization that has been established by the federal government with oversight of a particular industry. The role of the regulatory organization is to create regulations to ensure fair and proper business dealings, and enforce those regulations. Regulatory organizations differ from self-regulatory organizations (SROs) in that SROs are established to encourage self-regulation within an industry. SROs and regulatory organizations work in concert to reduce federal intervention in industry. SROs usually fall under the oversight of the coinciding regulatory industry. The Securities Exchange Commission (SEC) is the regulatory organization with jurisdiction over the securities industry. The SEC works with FINRA, the securities industry SRO, to ensure compliance with federal regulation and reduce intervention by the SEC.

Purpose and Mission of an SRO

A self-regulatory organization, or SRO, is an organization that is established outside of the federal government to oversee an industry through the establishment of regulations and industry standards. The goal of the SROs with oversight of the securities industry is to protect investors through the creation of rules that encourage companies to conduct business fairly. The SROs that are responsible for the securities industry are subject to the jurisdiction of the Securities Exchange Commission, or the SEC. The SEC is a regulatory organization (part of the federal government) as opposed to a self-regulatory organization. Securities companies that subject themselves to the oversight of SROs are less likely to run afoul of federal laws.

Jurisdiction and Authority of SROs

The largest and most involved SROs in the securities industry are the Financial Industry Regulatory Authority (FINRA), the Municipal Securities Rule Making Board (MSRB), and the Chicago Board of Options Exchange (CBOE).

Financial Industry Regulatory Authority (FINRA)

The **Financial Industry Regulatory Authority (FINRA)** is a self-regulatory organization (SRO). It is accountable to and under the oversight of the Securities and Exchange Commission (SEC), and it governs securities trading and investment banking firms. The FINRA promulgates rules and regulations for these firms and their employees and associates, and it enforces the rules. FINRA also settles disputes between member firms and settles disputes between individuals and firms. Anyone who trades securities must be registered with FINRA.

Municipal Securities Rulemaking Board (MSRB)

The **Municipal Securities Rulemaking Board (MSRB)** is a self-regulatory organization (SRO) tasked with developing rules for banks and securities firms to follow whenever they underwrite, sell, purchase, or recommend municipal securities. The MSRB is subject to SEC oversight, and while it generates rules for firms to follow, it is not authorized to enforce violations of such rules.

Chicago Board Options Exchange (CBOE)

The **Chicago Board Options Exchange (CBOE)**, established in 1972, is a securities exchange and self-regulatory organization (SRO). As a securities exchange, it focuses on facilitating the trade of options contracts based on indices, equities, and interest rates. It is the largest options exchange in the world, with most prices for options transactions being established on the CBOE. As a self-regulatory organization (SRO), it also creates rules for options exchanges and enforces them. The CBOE promotes growth, innovation, enhanced technology, and corporate responsibility.

Other Regulators and Agencies

Department of the Treasury/IRS

The **Department of the Treasury** (or U.S. Treasury) is an agency of the executive branch of the U.S. federal government charged with governance over the country's economic and financial affairs. This includes minting coins and currency, borrowing money for the federal government (e.g., through U.S. Treasury bonds), protecting the economy and financial systems from various threats, and—through the Internal Revenue Service (IRS)—collecting taxes. Accordingly, the Department of the Treasury and, especially, the IRS have an interest in financial markets, both because they are realms of possible financial abuse and because there are numerous taxable transactions involved.

State Regulators

In addition to federal agencies, state regulators play an important role in not only state securities laws administration but also protecting the public from unscrupulous dealings and offering businesses with an established framework for selling securities. Formed in Kansas in 1919, the **North American Securities Administrators Association (NASAA)** is a voluntary association of securities regulators whose common purpose is the protection of investors from fraud. All fifty U.S. states have membership in NASAA, in addition to other parts of North America. NASAA therefore is central to state (as opposed to federal) securities regulation. Besides providing education for investors to prevent fraud, NASAA provides licensing to firms and agents and enforces state law concerning finance and securities.

The Federal Reserve

The Federal Reserve (the Fed) is in charge of overseeing the nation's money supply, and is the central bank, in charge of all other banks and serving as the "lender of last resort." The Fed gathers information about various factors affecting the economy including the business cycle and the gross domestic product (GDP). The Fed then determines what actions need to be taken in order to achieve economic goals and objectives. The Fed's primary tool for influencing the economy is monetary policy, whether by altering interest rates, reserve requirements, or purchasing patterns for U.S. Treasury securities. The Federal Reserve Board uses monetary policy to adjust the money supply and interest rates in a way that will be most likely to maintain economic stability. In most cases, the Fed's goal is to ensure that inflation remains low because low inflation is generally a sign of a healthy economy. Additionally, the Fed maintains responsibility for the oversight of financial institutions in order to promote efficiency in banking and protect individual consumers.

Securities Investor Protection Corporation (SIPC)

The **Securities Investor Protection Corporation (SIPC)** was set up by Congress in 1970 with the Securities Investor Protection Act to protect investors in case their brokerage firm goes out of business. Broker-dealers pay fees every year to the SIPC, which are then set aside to compensate customers of brokerage firms that go under. Each customer is protected up to $500,000, although no more than $250,000 of this can be for cash holdings. And it is important to note that each account is not covered up to $500,000—if a customer has more than one account, that customer's total coverage is still only $500,000. Additionally, joint and group accounts only count as one customer. Notably, the SIPC does not have regulatory authority and is not responsible for the investigation of firms or suspected fraud. Rather their role is to protect the financial interest of investors when investment firms face bankruptcy, liquidation, or other financial issues that place at risk. SIPC covers securities such as stocks, bonds, and mutual funds. SIPC does not protect against loss of investment value due to market declines and does not cover investments not registered with the SEC.

Federal Deposit Insurance Corporation (FDIC)

The **Federal Deposit Insurance Corporation (FDIC)** is a corporation of the U.S. federal government established by the Glass-Steagall Act of 1933. Its goal is to protect customer deposits in banks from bank failure or bankruptcy. The FDIC insures deposits of up to $250,000 per customer per bank but only for member banks. Therefore, it is important for depositors to ensure that the banks where they place their deposits are insured by the FDIC. The FDIC also maintains federal regulatory oversight for member banks and assumes a critical role in resolution and receivership in the event that an institution fails. The types of accounts that are protected by the FDIC include checking and savings accounts, money market accounts, and certificates of deposit (CDs).

Market Participants and Their Roles

Investors

Virtually anyone can participate in financial markets, and these investors can be grouped into distinct, and sometimes overlapping, categories. One such category is **accredited investors**, who, as their name implies, are "creditable" in their understanding of investments and therefore less in need of defending from fraud and misunderstanding, and so less subject to regulation and oversight. "Accredited investor" is a technical term used by the SEC to denote certain high-income and high-net-worth individuals and institutions, specifically defined in Regulation D. Another category of investor is **institutional investors**, which are "entities" or companies that are involved in investments. This could include hedge funds, banks, insurance companies, and trusts. Institutional investors are the big players on the market. A third category of investor is **retail investors**, which can be understood as smaller, individual, or otherwise non-institutional investors. Institutional investors are more likely to be accredited investors (though some retail investors are), and institutional investors frequently invest funds contributed by retail investors (e.g., a fund manager investing funds contributed by individuals).

Broker-Dealers

Broker-dealers (BD) are people or companies that trade securities on their **own behalf** (dealer) and also operate as **go-betweens** for other clients (brokers). Broker-dealers must be registered with the SEC. Because brokers only complete transactions for other persons and dealers only transact business for themselves, firms that perform both actions are called broker-dealers. Broker-dealers facilitate trading for clients that otherwise would not have been able to have access to the market while, at the same time, trading for their own accounts. While the capacity in which the broker-dealer acts depends upon the transaction, occasionally broker-dealers act as both brokers and dealers when they sell securities held to their current clientele.

Clearing Broker-Dealers and Introducing Broker-Dealers

An introducing broker-dealer is a broker-dealer (BD) that does not retain a client's securities or cash, but instead "introduces" the client to a clearing broker-dealer. Introducing broker-dealers are usually smaller companies and often do not have the resources of a larger clearing broker-dealer. However, they facilitate communication and connection between clearing broker-dealers and clients. Introducing BDs also direct transactions that they may not be able to execute to clearing broker-dealers.

The introducing BD's main role is to attract new assets, not necessarily to manage them. They often hold seminars and other informational events to attract clients and perform other marketing roles. While the introducing BD is helpful to a clearing BD by bringing clients to them, the introducing BD cannot hold client funds or securities; thus, they are dependent upon the clearing BD. This situation is not reciprocal, however. Clearing BDs can operate independently of introducing BDs, but they benefit from increased transaction volumes that introducing BDs bring them.

Executing Broker-Dealers and Prime Brokers

An executing broker-dealer is a broker-dealer that accepts and enters orders for clients. If that transaction is deemed to be "in good order," the executing broker-dealer will enter the trade on behalf of the client. Typically, the clients with whom they work are average retail investors. Prime broker is a term that refers to specialized services that some broker-dealers offer to select groups of clients, often high net-worth individuals (HNI). These specialized services can include cash management, securities lending, leveraged trade executions, and many other specialized services unique to HNIs which may not be applicable for ordinary retail investor. Prime brokers and executing brokers often work together to service clients. Since the prime broker provides specialized services, they may facilitate the executing broker by clearing trades that the executing broker has placed on behalf of the client.

Investment Advisers

Investment Advisers Act of 1940

The **Investment Advisers Act of 1940** is intended to provide additional regulation for investment advisers, as follows:

- Such advisers are considered to provide advice and counsel through means of interstate commerce,
- The advice and counsel of such companies typically relates to the purchase and sale of securities on a national securities exchange or through the Federal Reserve system, and
- The volume of such transactions is significant enough to have a direct impact on interstate commerce, national securities exchange, the national banking system and the national economy.

The Act was largely the result of the stock market crash in 1929, which wiped out the savings of millions. As a result, the government felt the need to regulate the advice, counsel, and analyses provided to investors by investment advisers.

Under the Investment Advisers Act of 1940, an **investment adviser** is defined as "any person who, for compensation, engages in the business of advising others, either directly or through publications or writings, as to the value of securities or as to the advisability of investing in, purchasing, or selling securities, or who, for compensation and as part of a regular business, issues or promulgates analyses or reports concerning securities."

This definition does **not** include:

- A bank or bank-holding company;
- Any lawyer, accountant, engineer, or teacher whose performance of investment services is incidental to their professional practice;
- Any broker or dealer, provided that the services performed are incidental to the regular business as a broker or dealer and from which the broker or dealer receives no special compensation;
- The publishers of newspapers, news magazines, or business and financial publications;
- Those whose advice only concerns securities that are direct obligations of the United States;
- Any nationally recognized statistical rating organization;
- Any family office;
- Anyone else as designated by the SEC.

Municipal Advisors

Municipal advisors (MAs) are any persons or institutions that provide advice (in the sense of recommendation, not mere information) to municipalities (e.g., cities, counties, townships) concerning the issuance of municipal securities, usually municipal bonds. MAs were introduced as a technical term in the Dodd-Frank Act of 2010. This act required anyone providing such advice to municipalities to register with the SEC and adhere to specific requirements. Notably, the municipal advisor has a strict fiduciary responsibility to the governmental entities which they serve. The act also forbade MAs from simultaneously providing underwriting services for the bonds they advised municipalities to issue. This designation frequently applies to broker-dealers but was created especially for the regulation of financial advisors who, in their municipal advice, were previously unregulated.

Issuers and Underwriters

The Securities Act of 1933 defines an issuer as "every person who issues or proposes to issue any security." The term "person" is broadly defined as "an individual, a corporation, a partnership, an association, a joint-stock company, a trust, any unincorporated organization, or a government or political subdivision thereof." The issuer plays a key role in the securities markets because the return to the investor, whether through capital appreciation and dividends on equity securities or through coupon and principal repayments on debt securities, will be dependent on the financial performance of the issuer. For example, if a company decides to issue shares of their common stock or bonds payable on a public exchange, the company is the issuer of the security.

An underwriter is defined as "any person who has purchased from an issuer with a view to, or offers or sells for an issuer with, the distribution of any security." Underwriters are primarily utilized by issuers in the primary distribution of securities. The role of the underwriter is to determine the initial pricing and to coordinate the sale and distribution of the security into the market. Underwriters are often also involved in the preparation of the necessary SEC filings and approvals.

Traders and Market Makers

Participants in financial markets can be either traders or investors. Whether as buyer or seller, **traders** tend to engage in financial transactions more frequently, aiming to analyze and profit from market trends in the short term. They often strive to profit by arbitrage, finding under-valuations of financial assets and quickly reselling them at a higher price for a profit. **Investors**, on the other hand, tend to engage in financial transactions less frequently and hold their financial assets for longer periods of time, paying less attention to the day-to-day trends of the financial market in which they are participating. A single person can be both a trader and an investor in different respects.

Market makers are brokers or broker-dealers who retain large holdings of specific securities and are on standby to buy or sell those securities according to the current bid/ask prices. Market makers play a vital role in providing **liquidity** for the financial markets by buying or selling the specific securities for which they are responsible when there is no general supply or demand, thus "making the market." They also promote general efficiency on stock exchanges by promoting ease of trading via their market making tendencies. While brokers typically handle market making responsibilities, the two business transactions are separate forms of business and must remain as such to prevent conflicts of interest instigated by a broker recommending securities based on the market the firm makes.

Custodians and Trustees

Both custodians and trustees act as fiduciaries for other people; that is, they are bound to act in the best interest of the party whom they represent. However, custodians and trustees act on others' behalves in different ways. A custodian's primary function is holding, or keeping in custody, the financial assets of their clients, which offers asset protection. Custodians frequently provide additional services, such as payment collection (e.g., for bond interest or stock dividends), account administration, and tax reporting. Trustees, on the other hand, do not necessarily store their clients' accounts but rather manage them. Trustees have more discretionary authority to make investments on behalf of their clients, having legal ownership but having a fiduciary obligation to invest such assets in the best interest of the trust beneficiary.

Transfer Agents

A **transfer agent** is a person or institution that acts on behalf of a corporation to keep track of investors and their activities, including account balances and account transactions. Transfer agents also help with the mailing and canceling of stock certificates and deal with any problems investors may have, such as lost stock certificates. Whenever transfer agents facilitate the transfer of a stock from one shareholder to another, there are specific transfer procedures which they must follow, as outlined by the SEC. Transfer agents ensure that any transfers of securities have been made in "good order," and that the securities have undergone a "good delivery."

Depositories and Clearing Corporations

The **Depository Trust and Clearing Corporation (DTCC)** is a clearing agency that clears and settles trades for broker-to-broker transactions through its subsidiary, the National Securities Clearing Corporation (NSCC). The Depository Trust and Clearing Corporation provides for securities certificate safekeeping by making all transfers of ownership via electronic transactions.

The **Options Clearing Corporation (OCC)** is an organization under the authority of the SEC and the Commodities Futures Trading Commission (CFTC), and its purpose is to serve as the issuer and guarantor of all listed options (i.e., all options listed on public exchanges). The OCC is authoritative over which options trade and the strike price at which they trade. Moreover, when investors decide to exercise their options, the OCC determines (randomly) which firm on the other end is obligated to close the option with the holder.

Market Structure

Types of Securities Markets

The Primary Market

The three types of securities markets are the primary market, the secondary market, and the over-the-counter market, which is further broken down into the third market and fourth market.

The primary market is the market in which securities are sold by the issuers to investors. This is the market on which initial public offerings, or IPOs, are made. Retail investors typically do not participate in the primary market.

The Secondary Market

Retail investors can participate in the secondary market, in which securities that have already undergone underwriting and the initial public offering process are traded. This occurs on stock exchanges. Examples of the secondary market include the New York Stock Exchange (NYSE), National Association of Securities Dealers Automated Quotations (NASDAQ), and the American Stock Exchange (ASE). The NYSE is an example of a physical market because it has a physical location in New York City where traders can physically trade securities. In contrast, NASDAQ does not have a physical trading facility and is therefore classified as an electronic market.

The Third Market

The other type of securities market is over-the-counter markets, or OTC markets. In OTC markets, trades are executed between individual parties without the oversight of a regulated exchange. Within the OTC market, there is the third market and the fourth market. The **third market** is somewhat of a mix of OTC and exchange-listed trading. It involves trading exchange-listed stocks, but with the trade itself occurring over-the-counter. This is often done for transactions occurring directly between broker-dealers and sizeable institutional investors, with the absence of fees and commissions typically applicable to secondary market trading.

The Fourth Market

The **fourth market** is like the third, in that it takes place apart from formal exchanges, but it is generally between two institutional parties, i.e., without the participation of a broker-dealer. Fourth market trading is closely related to "dark pools," which facilitate private financial transactions. The primary advantage of trading securities in the fourth market is the avoidance of broker related commission fees.

Economic Factors

Federal Reserve Board's (FRB) Impact on Business Activity and Market Stability

The **Federal Reserve Board (FRB)** plays a substantial role in determining the state and direction of the U.S. economy. As a network of regional banks operating under the authority of the federal government, the FRB makes decisions that have significant and immediate impacts on the stock markets and overall business conditions. They establish interest rates and control the money supply.

Monetary Policy vs. Fiscal Policy

Monetary policy is the means by which the monetary authority (central bank, currency board, etc.) regulates the money supply. This affects not only the growth and size of the supply but also, in turn, the interest rates. Monetary policy in the U.S. is set by the Federal Reserve Board (FRB). The FRB's policies are primarily executed by controlling short-term interest rates.

The term **fiscal policy** refers to the government's ability to tax its constituency and spend that revenue to affect the economy. In this way, the government is able to affect, if not change, the various stages of the business cycle. Fiscal policy in the U.S. is determined by Congress.

Monetary policy and fiscal policy differ in their purposes and, accordingly, in the organizations governing them. Monetary policy in the U.S. is set and enacted by the Federal Reserve Bank. Fiscal policy is legislated through Congress. Each new piece of fiscal policy must be voted on and passed in Congress, but monetary policy need not be ratified.

Open Market Activities and Impact on Economy

Open market operations consist of transactions to buy or sell government securities for the purpose of altering the amount of money in the banking system. In other words, open market operations are a tool utilized for purposes of monetary policy. Buying government securities places more money into the system, thus causing market growth, while selling securities causes contraction.

The Federal Open Market Committee (FOMC) is responsible for open market operations. The FOMC is a division of the Fed. As a means of controlling the money supply, the FOMC trades U.S. government securities on the secondary market. The FOMC buys or sells government securities depending on whether it wants to stimulate or slow down the economy. To stimulate the economy, the FOMC buys government securities on the secondary market. This puts money into the banking system which increases the amount available for lending. Increased money for lending triggers a decrease in interest rates and an increase in borrowing. To slow the economy, the FOMC sells securities. This removes money from banks which decreases the amount available to lend. This decrease triggers higher interest rates and a decrease in borrowing.

Different Rates

There are four important interest rates which influence the market:

- The first one is the **federal funds rate**. It is the rate the country's largest banks charge each other for overnight loans in order to satisfy their reserve requirements. It is the most volatile rate, and short-term interest rates throughout the economy are usually pegged to it.
- The **prime rate** is the one most people are familiar with: it is the rate banks charge their safest customers, usually large corporations with excellent credit. The prime rate moves up and down with the money supply set by the Federal Reserve Board.

- The **discount rate** is the interest rate the Federal Reserve Board charges to Federal Reserve Banks (i.e., member banks) for short-term loans.
- The **broker loan rate** is the rate that banks charge brokers and dealers when they lend them money for their customer's margin accounts. It is also known as the call loan rate, or call money rate.

Business Economic Factors

Purpose of Financial Statements

Financial statements are transcribed reports of a company's operating performance and financial position. Investors use financial statements to make informed decisions about investing in those companies. There are three primary financial statements: the income statement, the balance sheet, and the statement of cash flows. These statements are part of the documents that public companies are required to publish to investors every quarter.

- The **income statement**, or profit and loss (P&L) statement, reports revenue earned during a specified time period compared with the expenses incurred to generate the periodic revenue. It helps the investor determine whether or not the company turned a profit over a period of time based on their business operations.
  - **Net profit margin** is the ratio of profit to revenue (net profit/gross revenue) for a business. Net profit margin computes the percentage of every dollar earned that translates into profit. If net profit margin is compared across a group of companies in the same industry, it can be used to evaluate the effectiveness of current management at each company.
- The **balance sheet**, also called the statement of financial position, is a summated report of a company's assets, liabilities, and stockholder equity. It can be summarized with the following equation: assets = liabilities + stockholder equity. From this information, an investor should be able to ascertain a clear picture regarding the company's assets, how much (if any) money is owed, and the amount invested by owners or shareholders at a given point in time. The balance sheet is often used to evaluate an entity's liquidity or solvency, that is their ability to satisfy their debts over the short-term and long-term, respectively.
  - A company's **price-to-earnings ratio** (P/E ratio) is calculated by dividing its current share price by its earnings per share (EPS):

$$P/E = \frac{\text{Price per share}}{\text{Earnings per share}}$$

  - **Current ratio** is a measure of a company's short-term solvency and is calculated as current assets divided by current liabilities. Current assets are cash or assets that will be liquid within a year. Current liabilities are debts that will be due within a year.

$$\text{Current ratio} = \frac{\text{Current assets}}{\text{Current liabilities}}$$

  - **Book value** is found by subtracting a company's total assets by its total liabilities. Book value is an attempt to quantify the total dollar amount that would be paid out to stockholders if the company were liquidated.
  - **Acquisition value** refers to the cost of acquiring of an asset, including all fees, charges, and reasonable expenses incurred.

- The **statement of cash flows** is the financial statement that details a company's uses and sources of cash based on activity classification. Cash flows are divided between operating activities, investing activities, and financing activities. An analysis of the statement of cash flows can reveal how the company is managing long-term assets, whether they are generating adequate cash flow from their core business activities, and how the business is being financed through debt and equity transactions.

Business Cycle

The business cycle is a recurring but irregular series of movements in a nation's economy. A business cycle has four stages which are influenced by movements in the GDP as well as various other economic factors. The four stages include expansion, a peak, contraction, and a trough.

- Expansion is categorized by an increase in economic productivity, demonstrated by a rising GDP and increased consumer demand.
- A peak occurs when an economy achieves its maximum output capacity.
- Contraction is categorized by a decrease in economic productivity, indicated by a decreasing GDP and rising levels of unemployment.
- A trough occurs when the economy reaches its lowest possible level of production.

Indicators

Economists use a variety of techniques to measure economic conditions and determine where the economy is within the business cycle (expansion, peak, contraction, or trough).

- **Leading indicators** have predictive value and tend to point towards the economy's future. Changes in leading indicators can signal a recession or an expansion. Some leading indicators include the number of new houses being constructed, the amount of inventory the manufacturers of durable goods have on hand, and the stock market trends.
- **Lagging indicators**, as the name implies, take a while to reflect the changes in economic conditions. However, once they change to reflect the current conditions, they support the notion that the economy is either improving or declining. Lagging indicators include but are not limited to earnings and profits of major corporations, rising or falling numbers of unemployment compensation claims being filed, rising or falling wages, a change in the ratio of credit to income on the part of consumers, and a change in **inflation** as usually measured by the **Consumer Price Index** (CPI).
- **Coincident indicators** reflect the current status of the economy by varying directly with economic shifts. Examples of coincident indicators might include production rates, employee turnover, and earnings trends.

Basic Effects on Bond and Equity Markets

In order to better predict the performance of a company's stock, analysts place companies into one of three industry categories: growth, cyclical and defensive. Each category experiences a different degree of economic impact affecting a company's earnings.

- A growth industry experiences a higher and faster degree of growth in comparison with the rest of the economy. An example of a growth industry includes the technological sector.
- A company that is categorized as a cyclical industry behaves in accordance with the overall stock market. Cyclical industries include raw materials and manufacturing. Cyclical industries perform well when the economy performs well, and they perform poorly when the economy performs poorly.

- Defensive industries are nearly immune to changes in the overall market. Commodities produced in the defensive industry are considered necessities and people will not alter their purchasing behavior as a result of economic changes. Examples of defensive industries include pharmaceuticals and food.

Principal Economic Theories

Keynesian economic theory is named for John Maynard Keynes, a very influential economist of the twentieth century. Keynes taught that continued demand is what keeps the economy going, as demand for products leads to more businesses being opened, more jobs created, more money loaned, rising wages, etc. Based on that belief, he said it is the job of the federal government to keep the economy stable by spending tax money on government projects designed to stimulate certain sectors of the economy or to stimulate the economy as a whole. In Keynesian theory, big government spending is not only good, but actually necessary, for a healthy economy.

Monetarist economic theory is the brainchild of economist Milton Friedman. Friedman taught that inflation and deflation do not randomly occur but are the direct result of the amount of the money supply. When there is not enough money in circulation, prices fall. When there is too much money in circulation, people have more dollars to bid against each other for goods and services, so prices rise.

Friedman's theory suggests that it is the job of the federal government to carefully regulate the money supply, so as not to cause disruptions in the economy, but perhaps most importantly, that the government should otherwise stay out of the market. Monetarists believe that the money supply should increase, but only gradually. This is intended to keep demand for goods and services without increasing the risk of substantial inflation.

International Economic Factors

U.S. Balance of Payments (BOP)

The **balance of payments (BOP)** for a country keeps track of all the inflows and outflows made for that country in a given time period. This involves a record of all the transactions made between the country and all other countries, tracking the dollar amount of all imports and exports, financial transactions included. A positive balance of payments indicates a net inflow of money, and a negative balance indicates a net outflow.

The BOP is more comprehensive than the *balance of trade* (BOT), which includes only tangible imports and exports, as the BOP also includes intangible exchanges, such as financial transactions, in the calculation.

Gross Domestic Product (GDP), Gross National Product (DNP)

The gross domestic product (GDP) is a measure of the finished goods and services that are produced inside of a country in one year. The GDP factors in both private- and public-sector consumptions. It also includes the country's net exports, business spending, and government spending. The GDP provides an overall picture of a country's financial health as well as its productivity. Yearly GDPs can be compared to gain an understanding of the degree to which a country's economy has expanded or contracted from one year to the next. The GDP is different from the GNP. The GNP, or gross national product, is a measure of what a nation's citizens produce regardless of their physical location. The GDP measures the production of everyone inside of one country's borders regardless of their nationality.

EXCHANGE RATES

An **exchange rate** is the relationship between any two currencies, and it reflects how many units of one currency are required to obtain one unit of the other currency. They change daily, and many different factors can affect them. This constant change in the exchange rate is known as the float. If the dollar is going down in value with respect to another currency, it is depreciating; it will take more dollars to buy one unit of the other currency. When the dollar is getting stronger, it is appreciating, and can buy more of the other currency. Because of the nature of exchange rates, and due to their constant fluctuation, **currency trading** can be quite profitable. However, it is also very risky, and not suitable for the average investor.

Exchange rates which change according to the supply and demand fluctuations within the market are referred to as *floating* exchange rates, whereas exchange rates pegged by the government as the official rate are called *fixed* exchange rates.

One of the ways in which exchange rates are modified is through the intervention of central banks. A central bank will either buy or sell a particular currency in order to alter the value of its nation's currency against some foreign currency.

There are two basic ways in which exchange rates affect the securities market. First, changes in exchange rates directly affect the value of securities for foreign companies. Second, changes in exchange rates affect the cost for domestic businesses to do business abroad, thereby altering the value of those businesses' securities in the market.

Exchange rates can themselves be affected by the prevailing market interest rates in different countries. A high interest rate in one country will attract lenders to lend money there, thus increasing foreign investment and increasing the exchange rate. The opposite occurs with lower interest rates.

Offerings

Role of Participants

Investment banker refers any institutions (broker-dealers, particularly) which help issuers of securities to raise money for themselves. They assist the issuers in deciding all the facts related to the securities' issuance (which securities, what quantity, what price, etc.). Investment bankers often also underwrite the issue of thé securities.

Most investors are familiar with secondary market transactions, in which a corporation's securities are purchased from another investor or a dealer. The primary market, or **new issue market**, is of critical importance to corporations as they raise money to finance their operations. When a corporation issues new securities (debt or equity), it can choose to issue through either a public offering or a private placement. In a private placement, all purchasers of the securities are qualified investors, such as banks, insurance companies, or large, sophisticated financial institutions. As such, the company can avoid many of the regulatory filings typically required. Alternatively, the company may choose to issue the securities through a public offering. To provide expertise in this distribution of securities and to ensure they receive the most competitive price available, companies will typically hire an investment bank to serve as an underwriter for the transaction. The investment bank will set the initial price for the securities and generate interest in the transactions to appropriately size the new issue.

If a municipality is considering the issuance of securities, they often seek input from a municipal advisor who provides guidance regarding the types of securities, structures, and terms which may be ideal for the entity.

After an issuer (such as a corporation or municipality) has announced plans to issue securities, the next step is to find an **underwriter**, someone willing to bring the securities to the public on the issuer's behalf. Because of the large sums of money and the financial risk involved, an underwriting **syndicate** (a group of firms that have banded together in order to lower their individual risk and investment) often performs the underwriting. Members of the syndicate must sign a syndicate agreement as part of a syndicate contract, or agreement among underwriters. The contract contains the official terms: how much each firm is obliged to underwrite, how long the obligation lasts, the person officially in charge from each member firm, and other important details.

An underwriter generally purchases a new issue from a corporation and then attempts to resell the issue to investors. The underwriter and issuer negotiate to determine the terms or commitments under which the underwriter will operate.

Types of Offerings

Public vs. Private Securities Offerings

A private securities offering need not undergo the vetting process of an initial public offering because it is not offered to the general public. While public offerings are sold to the investing public, private offerings are sold only to a very specific group, and the issuer may not solicit the investing public with their offering. There tend to be fewer regulations (therefore greater risk) of private offerings since they are not offered to the general public. Public offerings must submit to the registration requirements outlined in the Securities Act of 1933, whereas private offerings are exempt from such registrations. Private offerings are not as efficient at raising capital as public offerings, since they do not have access to the general investing public. This results in many of their investors being large institutions or groups of wealthy people with common investing goals.

Initial Public Offering (IPO), Secondary Offering, and Follow-on Offering

Initial public offerings, or **IPOs**, are securities offerings that have undergone the underwriting process and obtained registration. The proceeds of the IPO go to the issuing company. This method is often used to obtain capital to expand operations. A secondary offering is an offering in which a large number of issue shares are sold by major stockholders in a company. In a secondary offering, all of the proceeds go to the stockholders and are not normally used to expand company operations. Another type of offering, called a "shelf offering," displays characteristics of initial offerings but occurs after the initial public offering. In a shelf offering, the company selling the securities has already made an IPO of their company but chose not to sell all of the shares in the IPO. Their SEC registrations are valid for two years, and they may sell the unsold securities for up to three years. In a shelf offering, the proceeds go to the issuing company.

If an issuer has already had an initial public offering (IPO) and therefore is already present on a securities exchange, it can make an additional issue of shares that follows the initial offering: hence, a **follow-on public offering (FPO)**. An FPO can be dilutive, which increases the total number of shares outstanding for that company (and thus the value per share is accordingly diluted), or it can be nondilutive, which does not increase the shares outstanding. An example of a nondilutive FPO would be if certain senior shareholders sold off shares that they held privately, thus moving those shares into the public exchange.

Methods of Distribution

As it relates to distribution, there are various types of commitments to which an underwriter can agree.

- A firm commitment requires that the underwriter purchase all of the issuer's securities.
- A market out clause requires the underwriter to purchase all of the issuer's securities, but the underwriter has the right to back out of the agreement if any information surfaces that could cast a negative light on the quality of the securities.
- A best-efforts commitment allows the underwriter to purchase only enough shares to meet demand.
- A mini-maxi commitment requires that a minimum number of shares be sold or the underwriter has the option to cancel the entire offer.
- An all or none commitment requires that every single issue be sold or the entire issue is cancelled.
- A standby commitment is an agreement in which an underwriter agrees to purchase securities remaining after existing shareholders have bought as many shares as they want.

Shelf Registrations and Distributions

Shelf registration occurs when a company fulfills registration requirements for securities substantially ahead of the securities' issuance, up to three years. If market conditions are not favorable to the issuer for securities at a given time, they can invoke shelf registration so that when market conditions improve, they can issue the securities quickly. Issuers can also invoke shelf registration to register securities for more general, undefined future offerings. Shelf registration is formalized in *SEC Rule 415*.

Types and Purpose of Offering Documents and Delivery Requirements

Offering documents are disclosures provided by issuers of securities providing specific and detailed financial information concerning both the issuer and the offering itself.

Prospectuses are formal documents which brokers are legally required to file with the SEC. They provide information about investments being offered for sale to the public, giving information so that investors can make intelligent and informed decisions. Stocks and bonds have two types of prospectuses, preliminary and final. **Red herrings** are another name for preliminary prospectuses. They are called such, not because they are misleading (as are "red herrings" in logic and rhetoric), but because they include a statement in red lettering on the cover declaring that they are preliminary, and thus that some items might be subject to change.

The purpose of the **prospectus** is to ensure that investors have access and are provided with, prior to the purchase of a security, a minimal level of information that is necessary for the investment decision-making process. Such information within the prospectus includes a mutual fund's objectives, strategy, risks, fees and expenses, and past performance. The format of each prospectus is the same to enable investors to easily compare different investments.

All information that an investment company is required to provide to investors before they purchase shares in the company is provided in the prospectus. However, some investors and members of the public may desire additional information about the company beyond what's provided in the prospectus. This additional information, such as the history of the company, or a detailed financial profile, is in the **statement of additional information (SAI)**, and must be provided to potential investors upon request. The SAI is commonly provided on the company website.

An understanding of the fund's objectives is important to a potential investor because there is variation, even within the same asset class and style, as to how the fund seeks to meet its investment objectives. Freedom to permit allocations to other styles and to use risk management techniques and derivatives can play a significant role in a fund's performance and will be outlined in the prospectus where the fund's strategy is described.

Official statements of a municipal bond issue must be signed by an officer of the issuer, and they must contain all the information prospective investors will need to evaluate the bond. They will also include the terms of the offering; a summary; how the raised funds will be used; the authority to issue the bonds; any collateral or security; a detailed description of the issuer, including credit rating; the actual construction plan; the results of a project feasibility study; details of the indenture; legal proceedings affecting the bond; tax status of the bond; and financial statements, legal opinion, and consultant reports.

An official statement for municipal bonds is similar to a prospectus for other securities. Municipal bonds also have a *preliminary official statement*, which is roughly equivalent to a preliminary prospectus for other securities.

Regulatory Filing Requirements and Exemptions

Some securities are **exempt** from the registration requirements applicable to other securities per the Securities Act of 1933. This is due either to the **credit standing** of the issuer, which is perceived to be high, or to the **authority** belonging to a government regulatory agency. For example, in the case of fixed annuities, they are exempt because the insurance company guarantees them. Exempt securities include the following:

- securities issued by the federal government or its agencies
- municipal (local government) bonds
- securities from banks, savings institutions, and credit unions
- public utility securities
- securities issued by nonprofit, educational, or religious institutions
- fixed annuities and insurance policies
- notes, bills of exchange, bankers' acceptances, and commercial paper with an initial maturity of at most 270 days

Blue sky laws are state laws designed to protect investors from fraud in securities transactions. These laws mandate that individuals or firms selling new issuances register such offerings at the state level and also supply key financial information related to the security and the issuer. The security issuer is responsible to register not merely with the SEC, but with each state where the securities are sold. Blue sky laws compliment federal provisions and add another layer of protection for investors who may lack financial knowledge and thus be susceptible to securities fraud.

Additional Rules and Regulations

In addition to the content included in this chapter, those sitting for the SIE Exam will need to be familiar with the following rules and regulations:

FINRA Rules

- 2266 – SIPC Information
  https://www.finra.org/rules-guidance/rulebooks/finra-rules/2266
- 2269 – Disclosure of Participation or Interest in Primary or Secondary Distribution
  https://www.finra.org/rules-guidance/rulebooks/finra-rules/2269
- 5250 – Payments for Market Making
  https://www.finra.org/rules-guidance/rulebooks/finra-rules/5250

MSRB Rules

- G-11 – Primary Offering Practices
  http://www.msrb.org/Rules-and-Interpretations/MSRB-Rules/General/Rule-G-11.aspx
- G-32 – Disclosures in Connection with Primary Offerings
  http://www.msrb.org/Rules-and-Interpretations/MSRB-Rules/General/Rule-G-32.aspx
- G-34 – CUSIP Numbers, New Issue and Market Information Requirements
  http://www.msrb.org/Rules-and-Interpretations/MSRB-Rules/General/Rule-G-34.aspx

SEC Rules and Regulations

- Securities Act of 1933
  https://legcounsel.house.gov/Comps/Securities%20Act%20Of%201933.pdf
  - Section 7 – Information Required in a Registration Statement
  - Section 8 – Taking Effect of Registration Statements and Amendments Thereto
  - Section 10 – Information Required in Prospectus
  - Section 23 – Unlawful Representations
  - 215 – Accredited Investor
  - 431 – Summary Prospectuses
  - Schedule A – Schedule of Information Required in Registration Statement
  - Schedule B – Schedule of Information Required in Registration Statement
- Securities Exchange Act of 1934
  https://legcounsel.house.gov/Comps/Securities%20Exchange%20Act%20Of%201934.pdf
  - Section 3(a) – Definitions and Application of Title
  - Section 12 – Registration Requirements for Securities
  - Section 15 – Registration and Regulation of Brokers and Dealers
  - Section 15A – Registered Securities Associations
  - Regulation D – Rules Governing the Limited Offer and Sale of Securities Without Registration Under the Securities Act of 1933
  - 144 – Persons Deemed Not to Be Engaged in a Distribution and Therefore Not Underwriters
  - 144A – Private Resales of Securities to Institutions
  - 145 – Reclassification of Securities, Mergers, Consolidations and Acquisitions of Assets
  - 147 – "Part of an Issue," "Person Resident," and "Doing Business Within" for Purposes of Section 3(a)(11)
  - 164 – Post-filing Free Writing Prospectuses in Connection with Certain Registered Offerings
- Securities Investor Protection Act of 1970 (SIPA)
  https://www.sipc.org/about-sipc/statute-and-rules/statute

Understanding Products and Their Risks

Products

Equity Securities

Equity securities are those securities that represent full or partial ownership in a corporation. Securities are most commonly sold by corporations who are attempting to generate capital to run their business. Common and preferred stock are both examples of equity securities.

Common Stock

The vast majority of stocks issued are **common stock**. Investors who own common stock equity securities can calculate the percentage of their ownership in a corporation by dividing the number of shares they own by the total number of shares outstanding. The role of the common shareholder differs substantially based on the size of the company. For smaller companies, shareholders may participate directly in the management of the business. However, for large companies such as publicly traded corporations, the shareholders elect a board of directors to act on their behalf through a voting process. The board of directors assumes the role of corporate governance including the selection of executive managers, officers, or directors to lead the organization and make important day-to-day operating decisions. Common shares for publicly traded corporations are available for sale and purchase on stock exchanges such as the NYSE and NASDAQ.

Types of Common Stock

Authorized stock is the maximum number of shares that a company has been approved to sell on the market. They may sell them all immediately or hold them back for sale at a later date, or for other purposes, such as employee stock options. Holding stocks back is fairly common, and authorized shares often exceed the actual shares issued for sale on the market. Once all authorized shares have been sold, or issued, the company may not sell any more shares without getting approval from current stockholders, because the company charter must be amended.

Issued stock is the number of shares that have ever been sold and held, even if they have since been repurchased by the company or retired.

Outstanding stock is the number of shares that are currently held by investors and tradeable in the market. If no shares have been repurchased or retired, then issued stock is the same as outstanding stock.

Shares that have been issued and sold are sometimes bought back by the company. The stock that is bought back from the market and held by the company is known as **treasury stock**. The corporation may hold the stock for future use, such as employee stock options, or they may retire it for good. Stock buybacks are usually seen as an indicator of a company's belief in the strength of its value and are often followed by an increase in share value, as investors will interpret the buyback as a sign of strength. Even if the share price remains the same, the earning per share should go up, since the number of shares outstanding that will share in company earnings has been reduced. The rights that apply to outstanding stock still on the market, such as *voting rights* and *dividend rights,* don't apply to treasury stock.

Preferred Stock

Some corporations issue a limited number of shares of **preferred stock**. Holders of preferred stock do not have voting rights under most circumstances. However, there are financial benefits to owning preferred stock instead of common stock. If a company goes bankrupt, preferred stock owners take precedence over common stockholders when it comes to distributing whatever assets are available. Additionally, preferred stock usually comes with a fixed dividend paid on a regular basis, so that even if the owners of common stock don't receive a dividend, preferred stock owners will. Because the dividend is fixed, owners of preferred stock can depend on a regular income. Because of these differences, the prices of preferred stocks tend to rise and fall with relation to interest rates, and not with other factors that affect the price of the common stock.

There are many different types of preferred stock. Normal preferred stock pays dividends at a fixed rate, but **adjustable-rate preferred stock** has the level of dividend payment change periodically. These payments are altered according to a benchmark, usually the risk-free rate on U.S. Treasury securities. Despite the fact that these types of stocks can change in their return, they are generally acknowledged to be more stable than preferred stocks with a fixed rate.

- **Cumulative preferred stock** is preferred stock that gives the stockholder the right to missed dividend payments from the company. Should the company miss a dividend payment to owners of cumulative preferred stock, the company must make up the payment at a later date, as it stays on the books as a debt until paid. This is opposed to *straight (or non-cumulative) preferred stock*, which has a fixed dividend payment (like cumulative preferred stock), but if the company misses any payments, they are not made up later.
- **Participating preferred stock** entitles the stockholder to a portion of the profits that remain after dividends and interest have been paid by the corporation. These are so called because they permit stockholders to participate further in the company's profits. Participating preferred stockholders also have special rights should the corporation liquidate.
- **Convertible preferred stock** consists of shares that can be converted into common stock if the owner so chooses. The conversion price is preset, and convertible preferred shares tend to rise and fall in value along with common shares because of this feature. They also usually have lower dividend payments than other preferred stocks.
- **Callable preferred stock** consists of shares that the company reserves the right to buy back at a future date at a specific price. When a company calls a preferred share, it will pay a premium over the stated price to make up for loss of future dividends. This can also be called *redeemable preferred stock*. Callable preferred stock is ordinarily covered by a *sinking fund provision*. In the same way that corporations can repurchase bonds with a sinking fund, the same can be done for their repurchasing of preferred stock.

RIGHTS

Common stockholders can have varying rights associated with their stock ownership. They can have *preemptive rights*, which privilege them to purchase shares of a new offering before the public; they can have a *pro rata share of dividends*, in which they receive dividends proportionally to their stock ownership in the corporation; they can have *access to corporate books*, where they gain information about the corporation's operations to which the public (and other shareholders) are not privy; and they can have various *voting powers* to influence the direction of the corporation.

A **preemptive right** is the right of a shareholder (though not of just any shareholder) to maintain their current percentage of share ownership in case the corporation decides to issue more stock. If a company decides to issue more stock, the company must give these privileged shareholders first crack at buying the shares before the company offers the shares to the general market (and usually below market price). Current shareholders will receive a subscription rights certificate, which will spell out the terms and conditions of the offer, such as the date, price, and how many shares they're entitled to buy based on their current ownership.

Common stockholders can have varying levels of **voting powers**. While most preferred stock does not include voting rights, most common stock does.

Common stockholders generally get one vote for each share they own per issue to be decided. For instance, a stockholder owning 1,000 shares in a corporation, voting for candidates to fill 5 different positions on the board of directors, will have a total of 5,000 votes to expend. However, corporations can facilitate different kinds of voting, which explain how these votes can be expended.

- *Statutory voting* requires the stockholder to split up his votes evenly among the issues being voted on. For instance, the above shareholder will have 1,000 votes maximum to expend on each of the 5 different positions being filled.
- *Cumulative voting*, on the other hand, does not require stockholders to split up their votes evenly. They are free to distribute their votes as they please. For instance, the above shareholder, if they wanted, could use all 5,000 of their votes on one particular candidate running for a singular position on the board of directors.

Since it is often inconvenient for all common stockholders to physically attend annual corporate meetings, they can still exercise their voting rights by hiring *proxies*, agents legally enabled to vote on the stockholders' behalf.

Warrants

Warrants are the right to buy a stock at a specified price, which is almost always higher than the price the stock is trading at when the warrant is issued. If the stock price rises above the warrant price, the warrant becomes very valuable, much like a call option, as the warrant owner has the right to purchase stock below the market price. The owner may choose to exercise the warrant and buy the stock, may sell the warrant, or may continue to hold it hoping the stock goes even higher, until the expiration date. Most warrants are good for five years.

American Depositary Receipts (ADRs)

An **American Depositary Receipt** (ADR) is a financial instrument created so that the stocks of foreign companies can be bought and sold on stock markets in the United States. Each ADR represents a certain number of shares of a foreign company, usually somewhere between one and ten shares. Each individual share is known as an American Depositary Share. ADRs are bought and sold just like other common stocks listed on the exchanges, and ADR owners have the same rights as other stockholders, including voting and receiving dividends, which are paid in dollars. An ADR is technically owned by a bank, which handles the ADR, and it is held in the buyer's name. An ADR can fluctuate in value due to changes in currency rates.

Other Knowledge Points

In sole proprietorships or general partnerships, the owners of the business are fully responsible for the liabilities which their business incurs to various creditors. There is a connection between the assets they personally own and their business, so that if their business goes under, creditors can lay claim to other assets besides what the owners have invested in the business. This concept is called *unlimited liability*.

By contrast, **limited liability** means that investors are not liable for all of the debts which a corporation has, but are liable only to the extent of their investment. While investors can then partake of the benefits of the company's growth, they are not subject to enormous harm if the company has severe debts or even bankruptcy. If a shareholder purchases $1,000 worth of a company's stock, then the investor's maximum loss is the $1,000 which they invested.

Rule 144 is an SEC rule governing the sale of restricted, unregistered, and control securities. (*Control securities* refer to securities that effectively give the owner control over the entity.) The rule establishes five requirements which must be met for the securities to be permissibly sold:

1. A specific holding period must pass. The seller may have to wait six to twelve months before selling.
2. An "adequate" amount of information concerning the securities' past performance has been publicly disclosed.
3. The amount of securities to be sold is no more than 1% either of the outstanding shares or of the average weekly trading volume over the previous four weeks.
4. A seller desiring to sell over 500 shares or $10,000 must file a form with the SEC prior to making the sale.
5. Other requirements for ordinary trades have been fulfilled.

Debt Instruments

Interest Rates and the Yield Curve

The yield curve is a graph that plots the interest rates of groups of bonds with similar characteristics and credit ratings but different durations. It will typically include bonds with terms from 3 months to 30 years. Yield curves are commonly characterized according to their shape:

- A **normal yield curve** is one that slopes upward from left to right. The interest rate at which a bond is available increases along with the duration.
- A **flat yield curve** is one that does not have a distinct slope. The interest rates for bonds of all durations are about the same.
- An **inverted yield curve** is one that slopes downward from left to right. The interest rate at which a bond is available decreases as bond duration increases.
- A **humped yield curve** is one that slopes upward and then downward again. The interest rates for short- and long-term bonds are lower than those of medium-term bonds.

The yield curve provides insight into the state of the debt market in the US. When investors expect economic growth and rising interest rates, they have less incentive to buy long-term debt securities, so the offered interest rates must be higher. This results in a normal yield curve. On the other hand, if investors expect interest rates to fall in the future, the demand for long-term bonds is higher since investors will want to lock in their interest rate before it drops. This results in an inverted yield curve.

Treasury Securities

Treasury bills (T-bills) are short-term obligations issued by the United States Treasury Department of the federal government. Like zero-coupon bonds, they don't pay interest, but are sold at less than face value, and the buyer collects face value at maturity. They are one of the main ways of funding the operation of the federal government, and they are sold in amounts ranging from $100 to $5,000,000. They have maturities of 4, 13, 26, or 52 weeks. Their prices are quoted in yield, which means that on paper the bid will be higher than the ask. Gains from Treasury bills are taxed only at the federal level.

Treasury notes (T-notes) are medium-term obligations issued by the United States Treasury Department of the federal government. Unlike T-bills, Treasury notes do pay interest, paying every six months. Proceeds from Treasury notes are used to fund the intermediate operations of the federal government. Their maturities range from one to ten years. They may also be refunded at maturity, with a new note instead of payment. T-notes are quoted as a percentage of par in increments of 1/32. Gains from Treasury notes are taxed only at the federal level.

Treasury bonds (T-bonds) are long-term obligations issued by the United States Treasury Department of the federal government. The proceeds from them help fund the long-term operations of the federal government. Like T-notes, T-bonds pay interest every six months. They are issued with maturities of ten to thirty years. For five years, from 2001 to 2006, the federal government stopped issuing thirty-year bonds. But due to popular demand by investors, the sale of thirty-year bonds was re-instituted in January of 2006. They are quoted as a percentage of par in 1/32 increments. Gains from Treasury bonds are taxed only at the federal level.

Brokerage firms and other financial institutions may purchase Treasury notes and Treasury bonds and put them in trust. They then sell the receipts, or rights to individual interest or principal payments, to other investors. These are called **Treasury receipts**. However, unlike the original treasury bonds and notes, Treasury receipts are not backed by the full faith and credit of the U.S. government.

STRIPS stands for *Separate Trading of Registered Interest and Principal Securities*. STRIPS are much like Treasury receipts, except that since the government has authorized stripping the securities into separate components, STRIPS are backed by the full faith and credit of the U.S. government.

Treasury Inflation Protected Securities (TIPS) were created to attract investors by offering protection against rising inflation, which erodes the value of fixed-income securities. Every six months, the interest rate paid on TIPS is adjusted to reflect changes in the Consumer Price Index (CPI). When inflation is rising, the interest payment paid on TIPS rises; if the CPI were to drop, interest payments would be lowered. Because of this built-in protection, TIPS are sold at lower interest rates than other government securities. Any increase in interest paid due to the adjustment is taxable in the year the adjustment is received.

Municipal Securities

There are three main types of municipal bonds, categorized according to the way that the bond repayments can be financed.

- **General obligation (GO) bonds** are the first type. These are issued to pay for improvements that benefit a community but don't produce income. They are also known as "full faith and credit issues," because they are repaid from tax revenue raised by the issuing government entity.
- **Revenue bonds** are issued by governments to finance projects and facilities that are expected to generate enough revenue to pay bondholders back without resorting to tax money.
- **Double-barreled bonds** are revenue bonds that also have the backing of the taxing authority. They are considered GO bonds, even though they depend primarily on revenue generated from the project for repayment.

Municipal bonds often are sold by an issuer to an underwriter, who then sells them to the public. There are two primary ways in which the underwriter might do this: a competitive sale or a negotiated sale. A **competitive sale** occurs when an issuer presents bonds for sale at a particular price (along with other terms of its issuance), and multiple underwriters may competitively submit bids to acquire the bonds. A **negotiated sale** involves an issuer first selecting an underwriter and then negotiating a sale price for that underwriter based on his purposes in selling (e.g., The particular investors to which the underwriter ultimately plans to sell).

Special Tax Bonds

Special tax bonds are municipal bonds where bondholders are repaid through a particular tax levied specifically for their repayment. Generally, this tax will be related to the project which the bonds have funded. For example, an excise tax on tobacco might repay bondholders whose bonds funded some public hospital venture.

Special Assessment Bonds

Special assessment bonds are municipal bonds where bondholders are repaid through the taxation of the community which received the benefits. For example, if a public playground or park is built in some community, then the property taxes of that community might increase to pay off the bondholders, according to the likelihood that such people would utilize it.

Moral Obligation Bonds

Moral obligation bonds are municipal bonds where the municipality adds a moral pledge to repay the bondholders, with this pledge backed by a reserve fund established in case of default or any other failure to pay. This is merely a moral obligation, not a legally binding one; yet municipalities have an additional incentive to keep their word, since their credit rating would suffer otherwise.

There are numerous ways for municipalities to fund immediate projects with short-term (one year or less) debt securities, classified according to the means of repaying the debt:

- **Tax anticipation notes (TANs)** are issued for an immediate activity or project, which are expected to be repaid with taxes.
- **Bond anticipation notes (BANs)** are similar to TANs, except that the debts are expected to be paid off through the later issuance of bonds.
- **Revenue anticipation notes (RANs)** are similar to TANs and BANs, except that the debts are expected to be paid off through the project's own revenue.
- **Tax and revenue anticipation notes (TRANs)** are expected to be paid off with both taxes and revenues.
- **Grant anticipation notes (GANs)** are issued by municipalities who expect to repay the debts with grants from the federal government.
- **Tax-exempt commercial paper** is a short-term loan which gives the investor (lender) various tax benefits at the local, state, or federal levels.

Asset-Backed Securities

Asset-backed securities (ABSs) are securities which are backed with some sort of asset as collateral. The collateralized asset may include but is not limited to loans, leases, receivables, and royalties. Asset-backed securities offer an alternative to corporate bonds for many investors.

Collateralized mortgage obligations (CMOs), also referred to as mortgage-backed securities, are issued by private financial institutions and represent bundles of private mortgages. Although marketed by private companies, CMOs are usually secured with financial instruments from Ginnie Mae (the Government National Mortgage Association), Freddie Mac, and Fannie Mae, and so are rated AAA.

Mortgages are bundled by maturity dates into groups called **tranches**. In a standard CMO, all tranches receive interest payments every month, but only one tranche at a time receives principal payments.

CMOs are considered very safe because they're tied to mortgages guaranteed by the federal government, although they are not themselves backed by the government. Their yield is higher than that of government securities, and payments are received monthly, instead of every six months. There is a big market for CMOs, so they're usually quite easy to sell, although this isn't true of all of them. The more complex ones tend to have lower liquidity. **Prepayment** is a risk, and some varieties of CMOs have other risks that make them unsuitable for less experienced or less wealthy investors. All investors must sign a **suitability statement** saying that they understand the risks of CMOs before purchase.

Collateralized debt obligations (CDOs) are similar to CMOs, also being subdivided into tranches bearing different degrees of risks and maturities. The main difference is that they are backed by debts other than mortgages, such as loans or bonds.

Corporate Bonds

A **bond** is a debt instrument, or debt security. Unlike stockholders, investors who purchase bonds receive no ownership in the company and no voting rights. Bonds are issued by private companies, by the federal government, and by state and local governments (municipal bonds) to raise money for various projects, or for operating expenses. The value of bond fluctuates with interest rates, and not with the success of the company or the stock market. Should a company go bankrupt, bond owners are compensated before stockholders if there are any assets to be liquidated. For this reason, bonds are called *senior securities.*

The SEC generally classifies bonds based on maturity as either short-term, medium term, or long term:

- Short-term bonds have a maturity of three years or less.
- Medium-term bonds mature at between four and ten years.
- Long-term bonds have a maturity date exceeding ten years.

Investors should note that long-term bonds are considered to be riskier but are thus often accompanied by higher interest rates to compensate investors for the additional risk.

Corporate bonds are bonds issued by corporations. Whereas Treasury bonds can be backed by the full faith and credit of the U.S. government, corporations do not have that guarantee, and thus generally have higher interest rates. The maturity value of a bond is represented by the **par value**, normally $1,000. The **coupon value** represents the amount of interest the bondholder is entitled to receive for each interest payment period. The **yield** of a bond is often different from the coupon interest rate depending on whether the bond sold at a discount or a premium. Generally, bonds are discounted such that the selling price is equal to fair value based on the interest rate associated with similar securities of similar risks. Therefore, the yield represents the actual rate of interest that the bondholder earns based on what they paid for the bond which is not necessarily equal to its par value.

High-Yield Bonds

Since the riskiness of the bond is inversely related to the interest rates, **high-yield bonds** are bonds with lower credit ratings than usual corporate bonds (below a "BBB" S&P rating and below a "Baa"

Moody's rating). These are called "junk bonds," although they are still popular among investors worldwide.

Secured Bonds

Secured bonds are bonds backed by some collateral, such that if the issuer defaults, the bond investor has claims on the collateralized asset.

- *Mortgage bonds* are bonds secured by a mortgage on property owned by the issuer. The issuer would then have to liquidate this asset to repay the bondholder if the issuer defaults.
- *Equipment trusts* are bonds issued by transportation companies backed by the assets they employ, such as trucks or airplanes.
- *Collateral trusts* are bonds backed by financial assets, such as stocks and other bonds.
- *Guaranteed bonds* are bonds backed by the promise of a firm besides the issuer, ordinarily a parent company.

In the case of trusts, the collateralized assets are under the authority of a third-party trustee.

Convertible Bonds

Convertible bonds are bonds that can be converted into a stated number of shares of the issuing company's stock. This makes them attractive to investors because they combine features of both financial instruments—they pay interest, which is regular income, and they can also appreciate if the company's stock appreciates. If the stock goes up, the holder of a convertible bond can choose to convert them to stocks, or sell the bond on the market, and receive a premium to reflect the appreciation of the stock.

Some convertible bonds give the issuer the right to *force conversions*, forcing bondholders to convert their convertible bonds into stock. Companies who force conversions usually do so to refinance their bonds if a lower interest rate is available.

Parity occurs when a convertible bond is trading on the market for the same price as the stock to which it can be converted.

The **conversion ratio** gives the number of shares a convertible bond may be converted into. It is calculated by the following formula:

Conversion ratio = (par value of bond) / (conversion price of stock)

For instance, for a bond with a par value of $1,000 and a conversion price of $20, the conversion ratio would be 50 shares.

Since the **parity price** of the bond is the price equivalent to the value of the underlying stock, its formula is as follows:

Parity price = (market price of stock) x (conversion ratio)

For instance, if the conversion ratio is 50 shares, and if the stock is trading on the market at $22/share, then the parity price of the bond would be $1,100 (a premium of $100 over par).

Bond Indentures

For any bond, the interest rate, frequency of interest payments, maturity date, characteristics of the bond (e.g., convertibility, callability), and the principal amount need to be disclosed in a contract between the bond issuer and the bond buyer. This contract is called an **indenture**.

Flat Trades for Bonds

A **flat trade** for a bond occurs if the bond is traded to another investor without accrued interest being included in the price. This can occur either because no interest has actually generated, or because the bond is in default.

Compare this with the meaning of "flat trades" for equity securities, which has the related meaning of "breaking even." A stock trades flat if it is sold for the same price at which it was purchased.

Term Bonds and Serial Bonds

Any particular bond always has a particular maturity date, but bond issuers can attempt to strategically issue bonds of different durations for the sake of financing their own activities. **Term bonds** are bonds of the same issuance which have the same maturity date, whereas **serial bonds** mature at different (though regular) intervals.

Bond Ratings

Many bonds are rated by **bond rating companies**. The three best known are *Moody's*, *Standard & Poor's*, and *Fitch*. These companies assign ratings to bonds based on their evaluation of the creditworthiness of the bond issuer. They evaluate such things as how much debt the company has and the company's ability to manage it, how much cash flow the company can reasonably expect, and the history and performance of the company and its managers at handling debt. As a company's circumstances change, their bond rating can be upgraded or downgraded.

AAA, AA, A, and BBB are labeled **investment grade**. Investment grade ratings are those rated greater than or equal to BBB- or Baa and represent a low risk of defaulting. The highest-rated bonds AAA, have the least risk of defaulting. Bonds with ratings equal to or less than BB, B, or CCC are considered **junk bonds** because they have low credit quality.

Call Provisions on Bonds

Call provisions are arrangements on bonds stating that the bond issuer has the right to purchase back and retire the bond. These provisions ordinarily establish a timeframe when the call can occur, including details on the price and accrued interest paid to the bondholders. Bond issuers will call bonds if the market interest rate is lower than the bond rate, so that they can refinance their bonds to pay less interest. Due to the risk this places on bond investors, bonds with call provisions have a higher yield.

A particular type of call provision is a *make whole call*, whose aim is to properly compensate bond investors for future interest revenues they do not receive because of a bond call. With a make whole call provision, the bond issuer will be required to pay a lump sum equal to the net present value (NPV) of the future interest payments at the time of the call.

Bond Refunding

Bond refunding is when an issuer sells a new bond issue in order to raise money to redeem a previous bond issue. This is done to take advantage of lower interest rates. Refunding becomes more likely as bonds get closer to the maturity date.

Pre-Refunding

Pre-refunding is when the issuer sells a new set of bonds at a lower interest rate but doesn't call the previous issue of bonds. The proceeds from the sale are placed in escrow and used to buy federal government securities, and the interest received is used to call the previous issue at the first call date. This is also known as *advance refunding*. Bonds that are pre-refunded have the highest possible bond rating, as the risk of default is virtually nonexistent.

Bond Liquidity

The following conditions affect **bond liquidity**:

- how *well-known* or widely owned they are
- the bond *rating* (higher rating means easier trades)
- the *quality* of the bond issuer
- how *mature* the bond is
- how high the *interest rate* is
- whether it is trading at, above, or below *par*
- whether it has any *call features*

Other Debt Instruments

Commercial paper refers to short-term, unsecured promissory notes issued by corporations to cover cash shortages brought on by various factors, such as large accounts receivable or seasonal business fluctuations. Maturity on commercial paper is generally within 90 days but can range anywhere from 1 to 270 days.

There are two kinds of commercial paper. *Direct paper* is sold directly by the financing institution to the public, without going through dealers. *Dealer paper* is any commercial paper marketed through dealers.

Certificates of deposit (CDs) are financial instruments offered by banks, having a specific term (such as six months or one year) and usually having a fixed interest rate. Due to the decrease in accessibility for money, banks generally have higher interest rates on CDs compared with other bank accounts.

- **Brokered certificates of deposit** are CDs which are not purchased directly from a bank, but instead mediated by a brokerage firm (or from some other entity besides a bank). These CDs are generally pricier.
- **Jumbo certificates of deposit** are CDs with a minimum face value of $100,000. These are, of course, ordinarily purchased only by large institutional investors, and they are considered to be low-risk.

A **banker's acceptance (BA)** is commonly used in international transactions. It is the corporate equivalent of a post-dated check and can have limits of 1 to 270 days. A banker's acceptance is better than a regular postdated check because the holder has the goods being traded as collateral in case the bank underwriting the acceptance goes under. Bankers' acceptances are bought and sold in the money market. They sell at a discount and mature at face value.

Auction-rate securities (ARSs) are a form of debt security where the interest rate is determined by a Dutch auction. (A *Dutch auction* is a "reverse" auction, where the auctioneer begins with a high price and keeps lowering it to some minimum price. The first bidder wins.) These debt securities typically have a long-term maturity, but in practice are treated as shorter-term, since the interest rate is periodically (e.g., monthly) reset through another Dutch auction.

Options

Terminology

- The **underlying instrument** for an option is the entity which the buyer of the option contract has the right either to buy (for call options) or to sell (for put options). If an investor purchases a call option to buy shares of ABC stock for $15/share before February 1, then the ABC stock is the underlying instrument of the option contract.
- The **exercise price** is the price at which the holder of the option can buy or sell the underlying instrument, regardless of the market price. (The gain or loss by the investor depends upon the difference between the exercise price and the actual price.) In the above example, $15/share is the exercise price.
- The **expiration date** is the final date at which the holder of an option can exercise the right to buy or sell the underlying instrument. After the date, the option expires, and he can only buy or sell the instrument at the actual market price. In the example above, February 1 is the expiration date.
- An option with the right to buy is a **call option**, and an option with a right to sell is a **put option**.
- The **spread** for a stock option is the difference between the strike price (that is, the price at which one can exercise the right to engage in the transaction) and the current market value of the stock.
- ***In the money*** means that the strike price and market value of the stock are such that exercising the option would be a gain for the investor. For instance, if a trader has a call option and the strike price is less than the market value, then he is in the money. The same goes for a trader with a put option, if the strike price is greater than the stocks' market value. Keep in mind, however, that an option can be "in the money" without necessarily being profitable, because the gain on the closing transaction also needs to make up for the cost of the option itself.
- ***Out of the money*** means that the strike price and market value of the stock are such that exercising the option would be a loss for the investor.

Types of Options

Puts and Calls

Listed options are options traded on an exchange, and thus are also called *exchange-traded options*. Consequently, listed options are required to follow exchange rules. Listed options can be classified as either *American style* or *European style* options, with European style options (the less common style) having a smaller timeframe in which they can be exercised.

Options are often divided into the categories of puts and calls. Simply, these categories imply the following:

- **Puts:** The person or entity holding the option has the right to sell a specific security at some point in the future assuming certain parameters.
- **Calls:** The person or entity holding the option has the right to buy a specific security at some point in the future assuming certain parameters.

Yield-based options are options whose underlying instrument is a bond. The profit or loss on these options is the difference between the strike price and the yield of the bond.

Currency options are options that give the trader the right to purchase (or sell) some currency at a specified exchange rate. This allows investors to profit, or especially to avoid losses, from changes in exchange rate, and is especially utilized by corporations to hedge the value of receivables or payables denominated in a foreign currency.

Yield-based options are options that give the trader the right to purchase (or sell) a bond whose value derives from its yield. The value of the option thus depends on any difference between the option's strike price and the bond's yield.

Equity vs. Index

- **Equity options** are contracts that provide the right to buy or sell an equity security, such as a stock, at a given price (the strike price), independent of the actual market price for the stock at that time.
- **Index options** are options whose underlying instrument is a set of stocks linked to an index, such as the S&P 500.

Publishing Option Information

Tables displaying options for sale list not only the security, date, type of option (call or put), strike price, bid price, and ask price, but also have a number of other factors which are meant to be useful to investors in evaluating options. These factors include *extrinsic bid/ask price*, which measures the time premium value of the option, the *implied volatility* of the option, and a number of Greek factors: Delta, Gamma, Vega, and Theta.

Hedging for Equity with Put Options

Suppose an investor has a number of stocks which have done well over the previous few years, increasing by 30% or so in value. If they are concerned about the price peaking and dropping, they can purchase a put option to ensure that they will not experience losses in selling those stocks should the price drop. This is called **hedging for equity**.

Yet, because determining and acquiring proper put options for each stock can be difficult or otherwise time-consuming, a good idea for the investor would be to purchase a put option on an **index**, so that the option varies with the value of a number of major companies comprising the index (and assuming that their investments are in these kinds of companies).

Option Premiums

Premiums are the prices paid to purchase an option contract, or in other words, they are the profits made by writers of option contracts. There are two main components to a premium: the *intrinsic value*, which is the value inherent to the right embedded in the option, and the *time value*, which is the value of owning the option for a particular duration of time.

As the expiration date nears, the time value of the option diminishes, in which case the premium, if it would be traded to a different person (i.e., if the trader currently holding the option traded it to someone else), would more closely reflect the intrinsic value of the option.

Cash Settlements

Using cash settlement, which is also known as **same day settlement**, the seller must deliver the securities, and the buyer must pay for the securities, on the day the trade is executed. If the trade takes place before 2:00 p.m. ET, then settlement must take place by 2:30 p.m. If the trade takes place after 2:00 p.m., it must be settled within thirty minutes.

Covered Calls

If an investor believes the price of a stock will go down in the future, the investor can write a call on the stock, giving the call buyer the right to purchase the stock from the investor in the future at a specific price. If the stock falls in price or stays even, the call writer makes money on the option premium. However, if the stock rises and the call becomes "in the money," the call writer will have to deliver the stock to the call owner. A call is **covered** if the call writer actually owns the stock which they are writing a call on. If the investor does not own the stock but would have to purchase it to honor the call, then the call is considered **uncovered**.

If the investor purchases the stock at the same time that the call option is written, then they are engaging in a "buy-write" strategy.

Exercising

Exercising an option is activating the right contained in the option contract. If a trader exercises a call option, they are at that point entitled to the underlying securities at the strike price. There are different rules governing the exercising of options:

- *American-style exercising* means that, at any time before the option has reached its expiration date, the option-holder is able to exercise it. There are no restrictions on when the holder can exercise it besides the expiration date.
- *European-style exercising* means that the *only* time when the option-holder may exercise the option is at the expiration date. Option-holders are prohibited from exercising these options prior to the expiration date.

Because American-style options give the option-holder a much higher chance of profit, they also command a higher price than European-style options, all other things being equal.

Long and Short Positions

There are different "positions" which investors enter into when they buy or sell option contracts. A **long position** is a position where the trader wants the price to increase, and a **short position** is a position where the trader wants the price to decrease. Naturally, then, every single option contract involves one person in the long position and another in the short; someone will profit from the price growing and the other from the price dropping.

For instance, if a trader buys a call option, then they are in a long position with respect to the underlying asset: they want its price to increase, so that when they buy it, they can then sell it for the higher price at a profit. However, the seller will be in a short position. If a trader buys a put option, then they are in a short position with respect to the underlying asset, since they want the price to decrease, so that they can sell high and buy low.

For put options, the buyer will be in a short position with respect to the underlying asset, but in a long position with respect to the option contract itself. The value of a put option increases as the price of the underlying asset decreases. The key thing to remember is that long position means that the holder wants the price to increase, and short position means the holder wants the price to decrease.

Position Limits and Exercise Limits

Position limits are restrictions placed upon the number of options contracts an investor can hold with respect to a particular security. It is possible for investors to hold a long position on one option contract, and then, with respect to the same asset, hold a short position on a different option contract. To limit the ways these can be exploited, position limits exist.

Exercise limits are restrictions placed upon the number of option contracts an investor can exercise for a given security in a given time period. For instance, an investor (probably an institutional one) might be forbidden from exercising 6,000 option contracts on a particular share of stock in the span of five days. Note, however, that the investor is not limited on the *total* options that they can exercise—only on the total number that they can exercise *for a particular security*.

Option Assignments

Option assignments are notices received by the writers (i.e., sellers) of options, informing the writer that the buyer has now exercised the option. Thus, if the option is a put option, then an assignment means that the writer is at that point obligated to buy shares from the option-holder at the strike price. If the option is a call option, then the writer is obligated to sell shares to the option-holder. (If the writer of a call option already owns the shares which they are obligated to sell, then they are said to be *covered*; otherwise, they are said to be *naked* and must buy the shares on the market in order to sell them to the option-holder.)

The exercise date is different from the **settlement date** for options, which is the date by which the actual transaction needs to be made. For options, the settlement date is one business day after the date when the option is exercised.

Options Disclosure Document (ODD)

Options are riskier than other types of investments, so before engaging in their first options transaction, investors are required to receive an **Options Disclosure Document (ODD)** that articulates these increased risks and their tax implications. For example, if the investor is selling call options, they could have an unlimited maximum loss potential. The investor must read and sign this document before their brokerage account is permitted to include options.

Packaged Products: Investment Companies

Types of Investment Companies

Investment companies are classified into three separate categories according to the *Investment Company Act of 1940*. Of the three, the most common kind is the **management investment company (MIC).** There are two types of management investment companies: open-end and closed-end. Open-end MICs are more commonly known as *mutual funds*. They are called open-end because there is no limit to the number of shares that can issue.

Closed-End Funds

There are two types of management investment companies (MICs)—open-end and closed-end. **Closed-end MICs** are commonly known as *publicly traded funds*. They are called closed-end because they issue a fixed number of shares. Open-end funds have an indefinite number of shares, but closed-end funds have a finite number.

When closed-end management investment companies begin trading, they issue a **fixed number of shares** that are available for purchase by the public, issued at the IPO price. These shares then trade on the secondary market, just like other securities. They may also issue preferred stocks and sell bonds. Unlike in open-end funds, in closed-end funds only whole shares can be bought (never fractional shares). The market determines the price of a share of a closed-end MIC.

Moreover, while open-end funds always trade their shares at their net asset value (NAV), closed-end funds, being subject to the forces and influences of the secondary market, can sell with a premium or discount to their NAV.

Open-End Funds

Unlike closed-end management investment companies (MICs), **open-end MICs** do not issue a fixed number of shares. When they register with the SEC, they do so as an open offering, which gives them the right to raise more investment capital by issuing and selling shares continuously. In addition, the shares of open-end MICs do not trade on the secondary market. Anyone who wants to purchase shares must buy them directly from the MIC, and the *offering price* is determined by dividing the net asset value of the MIC by the number of shares outstanding and then adding a sales charge. Fractional shares can be bought, not just whole shares. When a shareholder wants to sell, the shareholder must sell the shares back to the company, not on the secondary market.

Unit Investment Trusts (UITs)

One type of investment company is the **unit investment trust (UIT).** Unit investment trusts operate by issuing shares entitling the owner to a portion of the investment portfolio owned by the trust. These shares can't be sold on the market, but only bought back, or redeemed, by the trust itself. The trust is obligated to purchase them when an investor wants to sell. Unit investment trusts don't have boards of directors, and they don't have investment managers or advisers (and thus no fees for them). They usually invest in government bonds or in mutual funds.

UITs were created to be long-term investments, similar to mutual funds. One key difference between UITs and mutual funds is that most UITs have a termination or maturity date. On the maturity date, all securities owned by the trust are liquidated and the net value is paid out to the shareholders.

Variable Contracts/Annuities

Life insurance companies sell **annuities**. Purchasers of annuities are buying a regular payment from the company, guaranteed for life. This guarantee makes an annuity different from virtually all other investments. Purchasers make either a one-time lump sum payment or a series of regular payments, and later they are entitled to regular withdrawals of income payments.

Annuities can also have *riders*: provisions built into the policy but purchased as a separate entity, entitling the annuitant to additional benefits other than the usual coverage. For example, a life insurance policy could have, as a rider, an "accelerated death benefit," which permits the policy holder to receive some of the coverage before death, such as in the case of severe illness. The coverage provided by the company at the policy holder's death would then be reduced by the accelerated amount. However, in order to have this accelerated benefit, it would have to be separately purchased as a rider on the ordinary life insurance contract.

- A **fixed annuity** guarantees a specific rate of return. Investors' premiums are deposited into the insurance company's general accounts. Fixed annuities are not considered securities, because all of the risk is on the insurance company, not the buyer.
- **Variable annuities** are considered securities, because the purchaser is taking the risk. With variable annuities, investors' monies are deposited into an account separate from the insurance company's general account, and the company invests these funds. Variable annuities guarantee payments for life, but don't guarantee the amount of the payments or the rate of return on the investment.

No-Load Funds

Many mutual funds charge a **load**, or *fee*, to investors who participate in the fund. This fee goes to reimburse underwriters and dealers who market the fund to investors. But a mutual fund can choose to distribute its shares to investors without using underwriters and dealers. If they do so, and therefore don't charge a fee to cover their sales expense, they are known as a **no-load fund**.

In addition, a 12b-1 fund with a 12b-1 fee of 0.25% or less is also classified as a no-load fund.

12b-1 fees are fees paid annually on mutual funds, ordinarily between 0.25% and 1% of the fund's net assets, to cover marketing and distribution costs for the fund. Their name is based upon the section from the *Investment Company Act of 1940* bringing them into existence. When originally created, the fee was thought to help investors, since the marketing and distribution benefits presumably outweighed the cost of the fee. That assumption is more challenged today, however.

Marketing Load Funds

Load funds may market and distribute their shares through one of two ways:

- utilizing an underwriter only, who sells the shares to the investing public
- utilizing an underwriter who sells the shares to brokers and dealers, with the brokers and dealers then selling the shares to the investing public

In either case, there is a profit built into the process for all parties between the fund and the investor. Thus, the load is primarily used to cover sales expenses.

Front-End Loads and Back-End Loads

When mutual funds use broker-dealers or underwriters to sell their shares to the public, they must pay for their services. To cover these sales and marketing services, mutual funds charge a fee, called a *load*. Loads vary, but by law they cannot exceed 8.5% of the public offering price.

Mutual funds that use a **front-end load** charge the fee when the investor buys shares.

When a mutual fund charges the fee when the investor withdraws shares (instead of when the investor buys the shares), it is called a **back-end load**. Back-end loads encourage investors to invest for the long-term because the load decreases the longer the investor holds the shares. If investors hold the shares long enough, the load eventually drops to zero. Because of this feature, back-end loads are also known as *contingent deferred loads.*

Calculating Load

There is a simple way of **calculating a mutual fund's load**. If the investor knows the public offering price (POP) and the net asset value (NAV) per share, then they can subtract the NAV from the POP in order to arrive at the load in dollars. They can then divide that figure by the POP to arrive at the load expressed as a percentage. Likewise, to determine the public offering price, simply add the dollar amount of the load to the net asset value.

Dollar-Cost Averaging

Dollar-cost averaging is a popular method of investing in mutual funds. Dollar-cost averaging occurs when a customer invests a fixed amount of money into a mutual fund on a regular basis—every month, every three months, etc. It is popular because it requires no decision making, and because it allows the investor to buy more shares when the price is lower. On the other hand, if share values don't fluctuate much but trend in one direction, dollar-cost averaging can be less than ideal. When shares are trending sharply up, the investor's money buys fewer and fewer shares of something that's becoming more and more valuable. Conversely, when the value of the shares is decreasing, the investor is buying more and more shares that are becoming less and less valuable, and the investor has no guarantee that the value will ever turn around and begin rising again.

Classes of Shares in Mutual Funds

Although all mutual fund shares are common stock, and mutual funds do not issue preferred stock, there are three classifications of shares bought by investors in the funds. What separates the three is the amount of the sales charges the investor will pay, and the manner in which the investor pays them. **Class A shares** are bought with a front-end load, and the load can be lowered by investing in large enough amounts to qualify for breakpoints. **Class B shares** are bought with a back-end load, which decreases over time. **Class C shares** are 12b-1 shares.

Net Asset Value (NAV)

Net asset value (NAV) is the value of one share of a mutual fund. NAV is always changing and must be calculated every day at the end of the trading day. Although it is quite a complicated calculation, in principle it is very simple. The fund's total liabilities are subtracted from the fund's total assets, which leaves the net asset value of the fund. That figure is then divided by the total number of shares outstanding, which gives the NAV per share. Usually, when NAV is mentioned, it refers to share NAV, not fund NAV.

Costs and Fees Associated with Investments

Mutual funds have portfolio managers who get paid a certain percentage, and in order to encourage investors to invest more, this percentage decreases for higher investment amounts. The point at which the percentage decreases is the **breakpoint**. (Brokers and dealers are forbidden from making "breakpoint sales": sales that seek to maximize commission income by encouraging investors to invest just below the breakpoint.)

Rights of accumulation (ROAs) are closely related to breakpoints. Investors can receive the reduced sales charge (the percentage paid to the portfolio manager) if the dollar amount of investments purchased, when combined with the fund investment they already possess, surpasses the breakpoint level.

Letters of intent (LOIs) can be signed by investors to permit them to receive the desired reduction in the sales charge immediately, so long as they pay the remaining amount needed to reach the breakpoint within a given time period.

When a broker facilitates an investment transaction on behalf of an investor and then charges the investor some fee for providing that service, the broker is receiving a **commission**. However, when the broker does not merely facilitate a trade, but actually acts as a principal—trading securities using their own account—then the profit made on such a transaction will occur from an increased price on the security over the price at which they obtained it, a **markup**.

An investment transaction less the commission or fee paid to the broker, yields the **net transaction**: the transaction amount on its own.

When investing in shares, one can purchase different kinds of shares, organized into different **share classes** based on the privileges and rights associated with those shares. Firms can charge different fees based on different share classes.

Fee-based accounts differ from other accounts—commission-based accounts—since fee-based accounts compensate the advisor based on a percentage of the client's assets, rather than as a commission for transactions facilitated.

Costs and Fees Associated with Annuities

Surrender charges are fees paid based upon an undue cancellation of some account or policy, occurring most often with life insurance policies. The fee is meant to cover the cost for keeping the account on the books, and therefore is usually waived for individuals who notify the insurance company of the cancellation sufficiently in advance.

Mortality and expense charges are fees included in variable annuities. When a life insurance company provides an annuity to some customer, the company calculates risks such as the life expectancy of the annuitant and charges a fee based upon these risks.

Sales Charges and Expenses for Mutual Funds

Mutual funds contain a number of different fees and expenses, and it is important for investors to understand how each will impact their investment performance prior to selecting a fund.

- **Front-End Sales Charge**: This fee is imposed when Class A shares are purchased. If a fund's front-end sales charge is 5% and an investor purchases $1,000, then the investor will have $950 invested in the fund and will have paid a front-end sales charge of $50.
- **Contingent Deferred Sales Charge (CDSC)**: A CDSC is normally imposed on Class B shares and follows a declining schedule as a percentage of assets redeemed. For instance, assuming a CDSC of one percent in the third year and an investor redeeming $1,000 worth of the fund's shares, then that investor will only receive $990 and will have paid $10 in CDSC.
- **Asset Based Charges**: Mutual funds also charge an amount against invested assets each year that includes charges related to management fees, marketing, and distribution fees (12b-1 fees), fees to the fund's investment adviser, transfer agent, and custodian, and any other operating expenses. In total, these fees are referred to as the expense ratio of the fund.

Sales Charge Structure Within a Variable Life Insurance Contract

Life insurance companies typically deduct both a sales charge and a premium expense charge from contributions to a variable life insurance policy. The **sales charge** is used to compensate the broker who sold the policy and also to cover the costs of issuing the policy. The sales charge is limited by the maximums set forth in the policy contract, typically in the range of 3 to 5%. Additionally, the insurance company deducts a portion of the premium deposits in order to cover certain state premium and DAC (Deferred Acquisition Cost) taxes. **Premium tax rates** vary by state and are assessed directly against the policy cash value. Different carriers treat the collection of DAC taxes differently, as that tax is due by the insurance company and just collected, typically over time, from the insurance contract.

Municipal Fund Securities

Coverdell Education Savings Accounts

Coverdell Education Savings Accounts (CESAs), formerly known as Coverdell IRAs, were created by Congress to enable parents to help fund their children's future college education. For 2022, the maximum contribution per year is $2,000, and anyone is allowed to contribute (i.e., not just the parents), so long as the sum total of all contributions for one child is no more than $2,000. Contributions must cease once the child turns 18, but the earnings are not taxed if directly applied to the beneficiary's educational expenses. However, for 2022, anyone making over $95,000 per year ($190,000 for couples) can't give the full $2,000, and anyone making over $110,000 per year ($220,000 for couples) is not allowed to participate.

529 College Savings Plan Accounts

529 plans, named after section 529 of the Internal Revenue Service code, are another way, besides Coverdell Educational Savings Accounts, for parents to pre-fund their child's education. The parent or other person opening and contributing to the account is considered the account **owner**, while the person whom the plan will ultimately benefit is termed the **beneficiary**. Taxes are deferred on the money invested in 529 plans, the money is generally not taxed in most states, and it isn't taxed by the federal government when withdrawn if applied directly to qualified educational expenses of the named beneficiary. With the Tax Cuts & Jobs Act of 2017 529 funds became eligible to use for K-

12 expenses, not just college expenses. Contributions are not deductible for federal income tax purposes. Additionally, if the monies are withdrawn for reasons other than qualifying educational costs, the account owner will be liable for federal income tax associated with the gains. 529 plans along with ABLE accounts are classified as municipal fund securities.

There are two kinds of 529 plans:

- One is a **pre-paid tuition plan**, which allows a parent to purchase a certain number of units of tuition, "locking in" the units, which will be used in the future, at today's rates, thereby protecting against rises in tuition over the years.
- The other kind of 529 is a **savings plan**. Plans vary greatly state by state, but one thing they have in common is that, because contributions to 529 plans are gifts, there are certain restrictions on contributions. However, these are much more lenient than for Coverdell accounts. 529 plans generally have lifetime contribution limits rather than annual limits. However, participants should consider any potential gift tax consequences when planning their contributions.

Local Government Investment Pools (LGIPs)

Just as any investor can benefit by pooling their funds with other investors, government entities, especially local government entities (counties, cities, villages, etc.) can do the same. When they do so, the arrangement is a **local government investment pool (LGIP)**. LGIPs allow public funds across different municipalities to be pooled, with the requirement that the investments follow specific guidelines (as might differ from pool to pool) and allow for fund liquidity. LGIPs frequently have very conservative investments. Sometimes LGIPs are managed by private firms, but oftentimes their investment managers are themselves public employees.

ABLE Accounts

In 2014 the Achieving a Better Life Experience Act (or ABLE Act) was passed to create ABLE accounts. ABLE accounts are very similar to 529 plans, and, since they are placed in the same portion of the tax code, are sometimes called 529 A accounts. The main difference between the two is that ABLE accounts are intended to fund expenses pertaining to disability rather than only education.

The taxation of ABLE contributions is just like that of 529 contributions. Contributions are subject only to gift tax constraints, with the specific limit varying by state and often being extremely high. Contributions are not tax-deductible, although earnings in the account can grow tax-deferred and be withdrawn tax-free for qualified disability-related expenses (again, similarly to 529 plans). These qualified expenses can be for numerous things that help a disabled person live, including assistive technology for life tasks, employment skills training, housing, transportation, and (like regular 529 plans) education. ABLE accounts can be opened for individuals with a significant disability that appears before they turn 26 years old, even if the individual is over 26 when they acquire the account. ABLE accounts, along with 529 plans, are classified as municipal fund securities.

Direct Participation Programs

Direct participation programs (DPPs), also called *direct participation plans*, are flow-through investments. The profits, losses, and income flow through the DPP and to the investors directly. The DPP itself pays no taxes; only the individual investors do. This is often referred to as pass-through or flow-through tax treatment as the gains and losses of the business flow through to the business owners' individual income tax returns.

DPPs are organized as limited partnerships, and the two terms are often used interchangeably. Limited partnerships are generally involved in real estate, oil and gas, or equipment leasing. Limited partners (as opposed to general partners) put up the money, but don't manage the business, and they have limited liability.

One drawback of a limited partnership is that it is very difficult for a partner to sell their interest in one. Another disadvantage is that they're sometimes organized simply to create losses that the partners can use to shelter income from taxation, although doing so is illegal.

Types of DDPs

Limited Partnerships

A **limited partnership** must have at least one general partner and at least one limited partner, although they usually have more. The **general partner** has more responsibilities and liabilities than does the limited partner. The general partner does the actual managing of the business and makes decisions that are legally binding for everyone in the partnership. They may be paid for services as a general partner and may buy and sell property on behalf of the partnership. The general partner must avoid conflicts of interest with the partnership and must keep their own funds separate from partnership funds at all times. The general partner may not borrow money from the partnership (although the partnership may borrow from the general partner), and they have a legal responsibility to use the assets of the partnership for the best interests of the partnership. Finally, the general partner is personally liable for all obligations incurred by the partnership.

Real-estate partnerships, or *real-estate DPPs*, can invest in a number of different real estate assets, and thus these partnerships can be classified in various ways:

- **Public housing partnerships** invest in the construction of low-income and retirement housing. Since these housing programs are government-assisted (e.g., missing rent payments are covered by the U.S. Department of Housing and Urban Development), they are considered the safest form of real-estate partnership.
- **Existing properties partnerships** invest in properties that are already constructed, with the purpose of gaining rental income.
- **New construction partnerships** invest in properties to be built, aiming to make a profit in selling the building.
- **Raw land partnerships** invest in mere land, not purchasing buildings or intending to build on the land. Their aim is to make money on capital gains as the value of the land increases. These are the riskiest form of real-estate DPP.

Equipment leasing partnerships seek to make a profit by purchasing and leasing various assets, such as computers, trucks, or machinery. There are two main types of leases for equipment leasing DPPs:

- **Full payout leases** rent out equipment for long periods of time (often the equipment's useful life), so that the first lease is sufficient to cover the cost of the equipment.
- **Operating leases** rent out equipment for rather short periods, or at least for periods where the total rental payments do not cover the cost of the equipment by themselves. In operating leases, the same equipment will be leased out several times. Because of this, they can be riskier than full payout leases.

Oil and gas partnerships aim to make a profit through various investments involving the extraction of oil and gas.

- **Exploratory oil and gas DPPs** search new areas to find new oil and drill for it. This is the riskiest oil and gas DPP, and its activity is also called "wildcatting."
- **Developmental oil and gas DPPs** search for new reserves in areas near wells that are already extracting oil or gas.
- **Income oil and gas DPPs** purchase wells that already exist.
- **Combination oil and gas DPPs** involve any assortment of the previous three.

Tenants in Common (TIC)

Tenants in common (TIC) refers to an arrangement where multiple people share ownership of a given property. The property can be commercial or residential in nature, and the ownership percentages do not have to be equal among the tenants. Due to the nature of the property, such investments are not readily or easily liquidated.

Real Estate Investment Trusts

Real estate investment trusts (REITs) are a specialized type of investment in real estate that trade on the stock market, and which have special tax advantages for investors. By being treated as a trust rather than a corporation for tax purposes, investors avoid the double-taxation that generally occurs when investors receive dividends from corporations. It's referred to as double-taxation because the corporation has paid income tax on the earnings at the corporate level, and the investor then pays income taxes on the dividend distribution at the individual level. To qualify as an REIT, and thus to avoid being taxed as a corporation, the trust must do all of the following:

- derive at least 75% of its income from real estate-related activity
- hold at least 75% of its assets in real estate, government securities, or cash
- distribute 90% of its profits to shareholders

The 90% distribution rule is one of the things that makes an REIT such an attractive investment for investors looking for income generating options. An REIT is organized as a trust, but it is bought and sold just like a common stock on a stock exchange. Shares are sold to raise capital for large real estate projects, usually commercial.

Though REITs are like mutual funds in that they pool investors' money and distribute shares, they are unlike mutual funds in that they have a *finite number of shares*. Related to this, while REIT securities are originally issued at their initial public offering (IPO) price, they can also be traded on the secondary market; investors are not limited from purchasing REIT shares directly issued by the issuer. And since REITs can be traded on the secondary market, shares will not simply be priced at their net asset value (NAV), but can move above or below NAV, according to market dynamics and sentiments.

Types of Real Estate Investment Trusts (REITs)

Private

Private REITs are those which are not registered with the SEC. Thus, they cannot be traded on a national exchange. Normally, private REITs have a limited audience of institutional investors.

Registered, Non-Listed

REITs classified as registered but non-listed are registered with the SEC. However, they are not publicly traded on a national stock exchange.

Listed

Listed REITs are registered with the SEC and also trade on a national stock exchange.

Alternative Classification

Additionally, REITS are often categorized based on the following characteristics:

- **Equity REITs** purchase real estate equity, owning real estate and making profit off of rent revenue or capital gains when the real estate is sold.
- **Mortgage REITs** purchase various debt securities related to real estate, such as construction loans and mortgages. The income from mortgage REITs is therefore based on interest.
- **Hybrid REITs** are combinations of the above two, investing in both equity and debt securities related to real estate.

Tax Treatment of REITs

Unfortunately for investors, dividends from REITs are often taxed at the same rate as ordinary income. Yet, certain dividends are **qualified dividends** and are thus eligible to be taxed at capital gains rates.

Furthermore, some portions of dividends can qualify as returns of capital, in which case they are not taxed at all.

Hedge Funds

Hedge funds are private investment funds that are legally restricted to very wealthy individuals, individuals who have an income surpassing the requisite threshold, and at least a $1 million net worth. Hedge funds are, in essence, mutual funds for the super wealthy.

Hedge funds are similar in structure to mutual funds, but they are dissimilar in that they are unregulated (because private) and thus have a wider array of investment options. Hedge funds are characteristically *very risky and speculative*, using purchases on margin, short sales, and other higher-risk investment strategies to aggressively make a profit.

Hedge funds' riskiness seems to contradict their name, since hedging is the reduction of risk—but the reason for the name is that, when hedge funds historically arose, one of their main purposes was to hedge against the risk of a bear market by selling short.

Hedge funds have very limited liquidity, often keeping investors' money for at least one year.

For tax purposes, hedge funds will be arranged as limited partnerships, so that they will qualify as flow-through entities. The manager of the fund (or an affiliate) will be the general partner, and the investors will be limited partners.

Private equity consists of any equity which isn't quoted on any public exchanges. Private investments might involve funding a private company to develop new technologies, or simply to be more successful in general. Private equity also might involve purchasing a public company for the sake of making it private.

Private equity often involves investors with enormous amounts of capital.

Exchange-Traded Products (ETPs)

Exchange Traded Funds (ETFs)

Exchange traded funds are shares of portfolios that are issued by investment companies, and then traded on exchanges like an individual stock. They are similar to mutual funds in that the value of the security is based upon the underlying holdings, but unlike mutual funds, once the shares have been offered, no more shares are created. This has led to ETFs being referred to as closed end funds.

The underlying portfolios of ETFs can be varied and far-reaching. An ETF may hold a basket of bonds, precious metals, commodities, stocks from emerging economies, and a multitude of other securities. This makes them very useful to investors in that they can fill a need in a portfolio without the inconvenience of conventional investment methods, such as storing precious metals after purchase.

An index fund is a portfolio that is based on a specific index and whose performance is designed to track the performance of the index. The index may be a stock market index, such as the S&P 500, or it may be a bond market index, such as the Barclays Capital Aggregate Bond Index. The index fund allows investors to invest in a specific index without having to purchase all of the securities that make up the index. This is especially useful for investors who are not interested in the day-to-day fluctuations of the market, but who are interested in the long-term performance of the index.

Difference Between ETFs and Hedge Funds

An **exchange-traded fund (ETF)** is a relatively newer type of security that seeks to *replicate* the performance of a given index or commodity. ETFs are valued throughout the day just as any other security would be and typically have very low fees as the investor is not paying for active management as they would be with most mutual fund investments.

A **hedge fund** is quite the opposite. Hedge funds seek unconventional sources of outperformance by picking individual stocks or market movements to exploit. Unlike an ETF, which is valued throughout each day and allows an investor to buy as little as one share, hedge funds are valued much less frequently, often monthly, and typically require substantial minimum investments. Hedge funds also offer significantly less liquidity as investments may be subject to long restricted periods where the investor cannot access the funds.

The primary factor in deciding between these two investment alternatives comes down to whether the investor believes that the market is efficient, or at least close, or whether the investor thinks that active management can provide a superior return.

Exchange-Traded Notes (ETNs)

Exchange-traded notes (ETNs) are hybrid securities which serve as a mixture of bonds and exchange-traded funds (ETFs). As their name implies, they are traded on an exchange, although they also have a maturity date like bonds. However, with ETNs, the repayment of principal at the maturity date is modified according to the day's market index factor. Further, the repayment is reduced by investing fees. The value of an ETN, however, is not simply based on the market index but also depends on the creditworthiness of the debtor company, since ETNs are unsecured debt instruments. Unlike ordinary bonds, ETNs do not have periodic coupon payments.

Investment Risks

Definition and Identification of Risk Types

Call risk is the chance that a callable bond will be called, causing the bondholder to lose the stream of interest payments left until maturity. Because bonds are generally called when interest rates are decreasing, the bondholder will have a hard time getting a comparable interest rate with the money received if the bond is called. To mitigate this risk, in addition to the call premium that is paid, callable bonds usually have a call protection feature—a period of time during which the issuer may not call the bonds, usually five to ten years in duration.

Capital risk is the risk of losing all the capital one has invested, particularly for options and warrants. Such securities have expiration dates, and therefore investors can lose all their money at those dates. Purchasing investment-grade bonds can help reduce this risk.

Credit risk is the risk for a creditor that principal and interest on a loan will not be repaid on time. Bond rating agencies (e.g., Moody's, Standard & Poor's, and Fitch) help investors to properly evaluate bond investments for their credit risk.

Currency risk is the risk that investments will be harmed through changes in currency exchange rates. This type of risk is a problem for international investors.

Inflationary risk is the risk that investments will substantively decrease in value due to the devaluation of the dollar through inflation.

Interest rate risk is the risk that investments will be harmed through fluctuations in interest rates. This type of risk particularly affects bond and mortgage holders.

Liquidity risk is the risk that an investor will not be able to liquidate their assets when they wish. The investor may want to sell some particular asset, but there may not be much of a market at a price that the investor finds worthwhile.

Systematic market risk is the risk intrinsic to the market taken as a whole or to a market segment. It is the risk that is unavoidable in some capacity, the risk that cannot be diversified away. Since nothing is certain with investments, there will always be some market risk inherent in the system.

Nonsystematic market risk is the risk associated with specific firms, rather than with the market as a whole. This type of risk, unlike systematic market risk, is diversifiable.

Political or legislative risk is the risk that investments could be harmed through some political events or unrest, whether domestic or abroad.

Prepayment risk is the risk that an investment which depends upon some stream of fixed income in the future (such as a bond) will have its principal repaid earlier than expected. This would reduce the overall expected gain on the investment.

Reinvestment risk is the risk that interest or dividends which one receives from different investments have to be reinvested at a lower rate of return.

Timing risk is simply the risk that an investor might make some transaction at the wrong time, failing to minimize their losses or maximize their gains.

Management risk is the risk that bad management decisions or other internal missteps will harm a company's performance and the value of investments in that company

Strategies for Mitigation of Risk

Diversification

Diversification for portfolios or accounts is the possession of several varied types of securities, usually so that different parts of one's portfolio offset risks in other parts. Diversification is in contrast with **concentration**, which involves an emphasis upon some specific type of asset. Part of diversification involves **asset allocation**, where one takes an investor's portfolio and divides it into different categories, such as cash, stocks, and bonds.

Strategic asset allocation seeks to structure a portfolio for long-term investment (e.g., having fewer stocks for older investors, all other things being equal), whereas **tactical** asset allocation seeks to structure a portfolio in response to particular market conditions (e.g., decreasing stocks in the short term if the market as a whole is expected to fare poorly).

An important characteristic of a portfolio is its **volatility**, that is, its tendency to fluctuate in its returns or losses according to the market's own fluctuations. Generally, portfolios follow the principle that an increased chance of return comes with an increased risk.

A broker should also help an investor construct his portfolio according to the various tax ramifications of the assets in question.

Portfolio Rebalancing

Based on the method of investing known as strategic allocation, an allocation of the assets is determined based on the investor's goal, and to maintain that allocation, the investor will sell the gains in the highly performing securities and buy more of the underperforming securities to maintain the allocation. This process is called **rebalancing** because it maintains the balance of the allocation. Rebalancing is an important process to maintain the allocation of the portfolio; without regular rebalancing, certain asset classes may grow or shrink to the point that it effectively changes the strategy of the portfolio. An equity portfolio's bond asset class may overtake the equity allocation and change the objective of the portfolio against the investor's wishes.

Hedging

Hedging is similar to insurance for some type of investment risk. If an investor wishes to mitigate the risk involved with some security's devaluation, they can invest some of their other funds to "bet against" this security, so that in the event of its devaluation, any associated losses are not as grave. Besides security valuation, hedging can also be done with respect to interest rates such as interest rate swap agreements. The specific techniques employed in hedging will differ based on the kind and degree of risk involved in the particular investment.

Additional Rules and Regulations

In addition to the content included in this chapter, those sitting for the SIE Exam will need to be familiar with the following rules and regulations:

FINRA Rules

- 2261 – Disclosure of Financial Condition
  https://www.finra.org/rules-guidance/rulebooks/finra-rules/2261
- 2262 – Disclosure of Financial Relationship with Issuer
  https://www.finra.org/rules-guidance/rulebooks/finra-rules/2262
- 2310 – Direct Participation Programs
  https://www.finra.org/rules-guidance/rulebooks/finra-rules/2310
- 2330 – Members' Responsibilities Regarding Deferred Variable Annuities
  https://www.finra.org/rules-guidance/rulebooks/finra-rules/2330
- 2342 – "Breakpoint" Sales
  https://www.finra.org/rules-guidance/rulebooks/finra-rules/2342
- 2360 – Options
  https://www.finra.org/rules-guidance/rulebooks/finra-rules/2360

MSRB Rules

- D-12 – Definition of Municipal Fund Securities
  http://www.msrb.org/Rules-and-Interpretations/MSRB-Rules/Definitional/Rule-D-12.aspx
- G-17 – Conduct of Municipal Securities and Municipal Advisory Activities
  http://www.msrb.org/Rules-and-Interpretations/MSRB-Rules/General/Rule-G-17.aspx
- G-30 – Pricing and Commissions
  http://www.msrb.org/Rules-and-Interpretations/MSRB-Rules/General/Rule-G-30.aspx
- G-45 – Reporting of Information on Municipal Fund Securities
  http://www.msrb.org/Rules-and-Interpretations/MSRB-Rules/General/Rule-G-45.aspx

CBOE Rule

- Rule 1.1 – Definitions
  https://markets.cboe.com/us/options/regulation/

SEC Rules and Regulations

- Securities Exchange Act of 1934
  http://legcounsel.house.gov/Comps/Securities%20Exchange%20Act%20Of%201934.pdf
  - 3a11-1 – Definition of the Term "Equity Security"
  - 10b-18 – Purchases of Certain Equity Securities by the Issuer and Others
- Investment Company Act of 1940
  http://legcounsel.house.gov/Comps/Investment%20Company%20Act%20Of%201940.pdf
  - Section 3(a) – Definitions - "Investment Company"
  - Section 4 – Classification of Investment Companies
  - Section 5 – Subclassification of Management Companies
  - 12b-1 – Distribution of Shares by Registered Open-end Management Investment Company

Understanding Trading, Customer Accounts, and Prohibited Activities

Trading, Settlement, and Corporate Actions

Orders and Strategies

Types of Orders

Market Orders

Investors who trade securities on the secondary market must purchase stocks and bonds from other investors rather than from the issuer. Investors can make several types of orders relating to their securities purchase. A **market order** is a type of order that requires the investor's order to be carried out as soon as the investor makes the order. An investor who submits a market order will have the order carried out immediately at whatever price exists when the order is executed despite the price that existed when the order was submitted. A market order guarantees that the order will be executed. It does not guarantee the price at which the order will be executed.

If a market order is placed, the intent of the trader is to execute the order immediately at the best possible price. A floor broker will fill the order based upon the prevailing offer, bid, or ask.

When a stop order is placed, the order is not executed until either a lower or upper trigger price is reached. At that point, the order is executed at the next market price.

MARKET ORDER & STOP ORDER

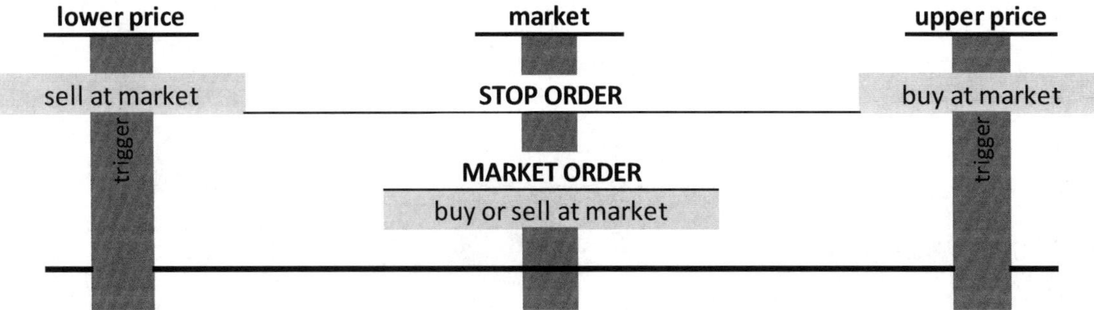

Buy Limit and Sell Limit Orders

A **limit order** sets a minimum or maximum price at which an investor wants an order executed. An investor will place a buy limit order when they want to set a maximum price to pay for a security. The buy limit order will only be executed if the price is **at or below the maximum** limit. If the price exceeds this limit, then the order will not be executed. An investor places a sell limit order when they want to set a minimum price that they will accept for a security. Like the buy limit order, the sell limit order is not guaranteed to be executed. It will only be executed **at or above the specified minimum** price.

Buy Stop, Sell Stop, and Stop Limit Orders

Buy stop, sell stop, and stop limit orders are all types of stop orders. A stop order requires that the investor set a stop price or trigger price. Once a stock price reaches or passes the trigger price, a stop order becomes a market order. The stop price in a buy stop order is set above a security's current price. When the price reaches or exceeds the stop price, the securities can be purchased by the investor. The stop price in a sell stop order is set below the current market price of the security. If the price reaches or drops below the stop price, the securities are sold by the investor. Stop limit orders combine the features of stop orders and limit orders. Investors who issue a stop limit order set two prices: a stop price and a limit price. The order is executed once the price reaches the stop price, but it cannot be executed if the price goes beyond the limit price set by the investor.

At-the-Opening and Good-Till-Canceled Orders

An **at-the-opening** order type is one that will be executed at the opening bell of the stock exchange. This order can be entered as a market order (meaning the trade will take place regardless of the price) or can be entered with a limit or stop price attached to it so that the transaction will occur only if the opening price is above (if selling) or below (if buying) a certain threshold. A **good-till-canceled** order is one that will stay on the books of the broker-dealer until it can be executed unless the customer chooses to cancel it before it is executed. This is helpful if the customer knows that they want to execute a trade once a certain threshold is met but does not know when or if that price will be met.

Stop Orders and Stop Loss Orders

These types of orders are used by customers who wish to avoid an excessive loss. Stop orders are also called stop loss orders. Stop orders require the investor to set a stop price. The **stop order** only becomes executable once the stock price has gone through the stop price. The stop price acts as a trigger—once a stock price reaches the stop price, the stop order is executed. Stop orders can be buy stop orders or sell stop orders. When a stock's price passes through the trigger price, the order is executed according to the customer's directions. Setting a stop price allows the customer to exercise a higher degree of control on a trade. The customer can set the stop price at the level they feel would best meet their needs.

Discretionary Orders and Solicited Orders

Discretionary orders are orders given by an investor that leave some leeway for the broker to exercise their own judgment. Oftentimes this is added to a limit order so that a broker can execute a transaction if it's close to the limit, e.g., within 10 cents of a $17.00 buy limit threshold. The main motive for discretionary orders, then, is to increase the chance that a desirable (even if suboptimal) trade is executed. Discretionary orders differ from nondiscretionary orders, which lack any such component of independent judgment or discretion.

Solicited orders are orders first considered and proposed by the broker, not the investor. If a broker supposes a given trade is a good one for the investor, they might propose it to the client, obtain the client's consent, and then execute that order. Even though both solicited and unsolicited orders involve (and require) the investor's consent, more liability is placed on the broker for solicited trades, particularly if the broker proposed a bad or unsuitable investment and if the proposal was unfaithful to their fiduciary duties.

Buy and Sell, Bid-Ask

A bid occurs when a trader proposes a price at which to buy an asset, whereas an ask involves a price at which to sell it. Therefore, the **bid-ask spread** is the difference between the two, specifically, the difference between the highest bid (or highest price of a willing buyer) and lowest ask (or lowest price of a willing seller). Sometimes the bid-ask spread is stated in absolute terms (e.g., in USD); sometimes it is stated as a percentage. When it is stated as a percentage, it is usually relative to the ask price, not the bid price.

Trade Capacity

When a representative works in an agent capacity for a customer, they are acting as a broker. Brokers work to find other investors that either desire to buy the security that their customer wants to sell or sell the security that their customer wants to buy. When a representative acts in a broker capacity, they are usually paid a percentage of the total transaction.

A broker-dealer that sells from their own inventory is acting in a dealer capacity. If a customer wants to buy a certain security and the dealer has it on hand, they may sell it to the customer from their stock of securities. They make money doing this by charging a markup, or an increase in the price that they paid for the security. Dealers may keep a large stock of high-volume securities on hand, both to better serve their customers with quicker executions and to benefit from the markups that they will receive.

Strategies for Buying and Selling Securities

Buying pertains to purchasing a security for an investment, while selling refers to the sale of an investment to another investor. There are strategies involved with each. Each may be done "at the market," or at the next available price, or they may have qualifiers attached to them that require them to be bought or sold at a certain price. The qualifiers are called stops and limits, and will trigger purchases or sells, or prevent transactions from occurring according to the investor's instructions.

The difference in selling long and selling short is that when an investor sells an asset short, they do not own it, and must borrow the security. They hope the security will decrease in value so they can buy the security at a lower price than at the borrowing price, and return the borrowed security to the lending broker. Holding a long position refers to traditional investing (buying and holding an asset in hopes of capital appreciation).

Investors should plan ahead and develop clear goals for their portfolio before they begin buying securities. Investment advisers should be aware of their client's time horizon when planning security purchases. The **time horizon** is the amount of time remaining before an investor *expects* to need to begin liquidating securities.

Long and Short, Naked and Covered

Uncovered, or naked, and covered positions usually refer to options positions. A naked position is one in which the investor does not own the security on which the option is based. Naked positions are much riskier than covered positions, because if the underlying asset moves in an unfavorable way, it could be untenable for the investor to cover the loss. For example, a covered call is generally considered the safest option to sell. If the value of the underlying security increases and the position is called, the customer only has to sell a security they already own. Uncovered calls, however, are generally considered the riskiest types of option. The value of the underlying security theoretically may increase infinitely, and since the investor doesn't own the security, they must buy it to meet the call, and they are at the mercy of the market as to price.

Bearish and Bullish

If an investor is said to be bearish, they believe that the market is going to decline soon, or that it is already in a state of decline. Bullish investors believe that there is a very positive outlook for the markets. Bearish investors may take steps to prepare for a bear market, such as selling positions short and selling their long positions to hold cash. Bearish investors may also buy assets that are negatively correlated to the market that they believe will decline. An investor that is bearish on equities will move funds to bonds since the two share a negative correlation. In the event that bearish investors do not want to sell their long positions, they may also use options to hedge their long positions to protect against loss.

Bullish investors tend to hold current investments hoping that they will increase. Like bearish investors, bullish investors write options, too, but with the intent of magnifying gains instead of hedging losses. Bullish investors tend not to hold cash, as they believe it can best be put to work in the market.

Investment Returns

Components of Return

A **dividend** is a portion of the company's profit that is returned to shareholders. A dividend can come in the form of cash, in which case a check is sent to the owner or to the owner's brokerage account. When dividends are paid in cash, they are considered income, and taxes must be paid on them during the tax year they're received. Dividends can also be in the form of additional shares of stock given to shareholders. These are not taxable until they're sold, just like all stocks. Because this type of stock dividend increases the number of outstanding shares, it decreases the market value of each share, but does not affect the total market value of the company.

Interest is the fee charged for the use of another's money. It is often expressed as an annual percentage rate (APR). Interest can also be simple or compound; compound interest periodically adds the outstanding interest to the principal, thus increasing the rate at which interest generates.

Tax-exempted interest is interest income that is not subject to federal income tax. Municipal bonds provide tax-exempted interest.

When an investor purchases shares and later sells them, the holding period of the securities decides whether they were a long-term or short-term investment. The **holding period** is the length of time the security is owned (i.e., the time between when a security is purchased and when it is sold).

Whenever an investor sells a security for more than he paid for it (the security's cost basis), the investor has received a **capital gain**, or a realized gain. An unrealized gain or loss, otherwise known as paper profit or loss, is a return that only exists on paper. If the investor held the security for more than a year, then it is considered a long-term capital gain, and is given favorable tax treatment; it is only taxed at 15%. If the investor held the security for less than a year before the sale, it is considered a short-term capital gain, and is taxed at the investor's regular income tax rate, which for most people is higher than 15%.

If the investor sells a security for less than its cost basis, then he or she has a **capital loss**. If, after adding up all the investor's capital gains and capital losses for the tax year, it turns out that the investor has a net capital loss, he or she may use that capital loss to offset taxes against earned income, up to a limit of $3,000 a year.

If an investor has an investment returned to him in part or in whole, such that he is not gaining anything beyond the original investment, then it is a **return of capital** (which is very different from return *on* capital). This is not taxed or considered as income, because it is simply a return of the original investment.

Different Types of Dividends

Cash dividends are the most common and are generally stated on a per share basis. For example, a company may declare a dividend of $1.58 per share of common stock.

Stock dividends result in the investor receiving additional shares of the company's common stock and thus require the company to issue additional shares to cover the dividend. The stock dividend does not affect the value of the company as it simply dilutes the value of each outstanding share. The investor is not required to pay taxes on the stock dividend until such shares are sold.

Stock dividends can be classified as small stock dividends or large stock dividends. The dividing line between the two is 25%. Stock dividends which represent less than 25% of pre-dividend outstanding shares are considered small, while stock dividends presenting more than 25% of pre-dividend outstanding shares are classified as large.

Dividend Payment Dates

Declaration date: This is the date on which the payment of a dividend is announced. Included in the announcement will be the amount of the dividend per share, the ex-dividend date, and the payment date.

Ex-dividend date: This is the date on which the owner of the security effectively becomes entitled to the dividend payment. Trades placed on or after the ex-dividend date would not be settled by the record date. If an investor purchases the security on or after the ex-dividend date, the seller (not the buyer) would be entitled to the dividend, and the security is said to trade ex-dividend. The ex-dividend date is usually the business day before the record date. Thus, if the record date falls on a Monday, the ex-dividend date would be the Friday of the previous week.

Record date: On the record date, the company determines who the current equity security holders are, as those individuals are the ones who will receive the dividend. When a publicly traded corporation declares a dividend, it documents the date on which an investor must be the stockholder of record in order to be paid the dividend.

Payment date: The payment date is the date on which dividends are actually distributed to investors.

Concepts of Measurement

A bond's **yield to maturity** (YTM) is how much return the bondholder will earn annually by holding the bond until its maturity date. If they are the original owner of the bond, this is the coupon rate, or nominal yield. However, if the bondholder bought the bond on the market, the yield to maturity (YTM) will depend on whether they bought the bond at a discount or at a premium. Very few bonds trade at par. Bonds bought at a discount will have a higher YTM, and bonds bought at a premium will have a lower YTM. Yield to maturity is also called *basis*.

Yield to call (YTC) is the bondholder's return if the bond is called before it matures.

Yield to worst (YTW) is the lowest possible yield for a bond without the issuer defaulting. It is obtained by calculating the YTM and the YTC for all the call dates and selecting the lowest.

Bond Credit Spread

Credit spread is the difference in value between two bonds with different credit ratings that are otherwise identical, with the comparison often made with a U.S. Treasury bond, as such a bond is deemed to be maximally secure. Credit spread is measured or stated in terms of **basis points**, each point equal to a hundredth of one percent, and all with reference to the bonds' yield. For example, if a proposed 5-year corporate bond had a yield of 3.89% and the corresponding 5-year U.S. Treasury bond had a yield of 2.36%, then the credit spread for these two bonds would be 389 – 236 = 153 basis points.

Annualized returns are a measurement of the expected return if an investor would have held an investment for an entire **year**. Annualized returns are calculated by multiplying the return of a security or portfolio by an annualization factor, or one year divided by the total number of days the security or portfolio was held. Annualized returns are useful measurements in that they can provide a rough estimate of expected annual returns of a security without having to hold the security for an entire year. However, investment decisions should not be based solely on annualization of securities as past performance is never indicative of future returns.

TOTAL RETURN

The **total return** of an investment includes dividends, interest, and capital gain, in addition to capital appreciation, evaluated annually. In this way, losses may be offset by dividends or interest. The current rate of return may not be accurate because of the discounting of these factors. This method is often considered to be the **most accurate measure** of how a certain asset may have performed for an investor. Investors assessing the value and performance of holdings should always take into account the total return of a security. What may appear to be an underperforming security at first glance may actually be a very good investment. Bonds are a classic example of securities whose performance is not shown in capital appreciation, and total return should be considered to provide a more complete picture of performance. The real value of the bond may be in the income it provides. Investors who are looking for investments with both growth (capital appreciation) and income (dividends/interest) are said to be prioritizing their total return.

RISK-ADJUSTED RETURN

Risk-adjusted return describes a measurement of the return of a portfolio or security that has been adjusted based upon the risk inherent to that portfolio or security. The risk-adjusted return is usually measured by the **Sharpe ratio**. The Sharpe ratio of a given portfolio or security is found by subtracting the risk-free rate, or the rate of return based on an investment in which there is little expectation of risk (usually Treasuries) and dividing that number by the standard deviation of the portfolio. The Sharpe ratio is indicative of the quantity of return compared to the amount of risk taken. It is important for an investor to understand the risk-adjusted return to understand that higher-than-normal returns may in fact be due to higher-than-normal risk, which could damage the returns of the portfolio or security at a later time.

COST BASIS

The **cost basis** (or *tax basis*) for stocks is the reference point to be used when determining one's capital gains or losses. If a stock's cost basis is $5,000 and the investor sells it for $5,500, then they have a capital gain of $500. Cost basis will often be listed as **cost basis per share**.

The cost basis for stock is not ordinarily the purchase price of the stock. When buying stock, the basis will be increased by fees and commissions paid to the broker or dealer.

If **dividends** are gained on stock and then reinvested in the stock, the dividends are still treated as income, in which case their reinvestment increases the cost basis of the stock by the amount reinvested.

Moreover, all reinvested dividends are still taxable.

COST BASIS OF STOCKS GIVEN AS GIFTS OR AS AN INHERITANCE

Stocks acquired as **gifts** will have a basis equal to the donor's basis unless they have decreased in value since the donor acquired them. In that case, their new basis is their value at the time of donation. If they have increased in value since the donor acquired them, the basis for the gift recipient will still equal the donor's basis.

Stock acquired by **inheritance** will have a basis equal to the value per share at the point of the decedent's death. All securities acquired by inheritance are automatically taxed as long-term.

Benchmarks and Indices

Benchmark portfolios are portfolios designed to mimic the **volatility** of the benchmark they purport to track. As an example, a portfolio benchmarked to the Dow Jones Industrial Average would reasonably be expected to rise 10% if the Dow Jones rose 10%. The same applies to other benchmarks such as the S&P 500 or the Russell 2000. Benchmark portfolios are often viewed as a product of the efficient market theory which is the theory that it is impossible to outperform the market. Benchmarked portfolios are often less expensive to manage and less expensive for investors to participate. This is because once the portfolio is indexed to the benchmark, little to no additional cost associated with investment management is incurred. Managers who actively manage portfolios often incur large expenses and pass them on to investors. This is usually not the case with benchmarked portfolios.

Market indices are numbers reporting an aggregate value from the combination of several securities' individual values. These indices are valued at a given date and presented in comparison to their base value from some earlier date. The securities which compose the market indices are selected so that the indices can report the market's performance as a whole. A prominent example of a market index is the S&P 500 Index.

Trade Settlement

Settlement Time Frames for Various Products

T + 1, T + 2, and T + 3

The **settlement date** in securities trading is the day that the trades actually settle, or securities change hands, as opposed to the execution date, which is the day the trade goes through. If a trade's settlement date is one business day after the execution date, then T + 1 applies; if two days, then T + 2; and if three days, then T + 3.

T + 2 is shorthand for **regular way settlement**. T + 2 is called regular way settlement because most securities trades, but not all, settle this way. Stocks, corporate and municipal bonds, and securities issued by agencies of the federal government all settle the regular way.

Physical vs. Book Entry

Securities used to be represented mostly by physical certificates, but **book-entry securities** (also called book-entry receipts) are only recorded electronically. These securities can be recorded in the **Direct Registration System**, a method of storing and trading shares. Trading electronically has the benefits of increased convenience, reduced time spent for trades, and decreased administrative costs.

Good delivery for book-entry securities carries different requirements than for physical certificates (e.g., a different requirement regarding mutilated certificates), according to the different nature of the transactions.

Good Delivery

Good delivery involves the requirements that must be met for a security in a transaction to be transferred to a buyer. A **security certificate** meeting these requirements is ready to be transferred "on good delivery." Otherwise, the trade cannot be settled.

Some of the general requirements for good delivery are that the certificate must be in good physical condition (i.e., not mutilated), that the certificate must have an endorsement, that the exact number of securities (whether shares or bonds) must be delivered, and that the correct currency denomination for the certificates must be delivered.

Good Delivery Requirements for Bonds

Bearer bonds (a.k.a. coupon bonds), which are not registered to particular individuals, but are as tradeable and liquid as dollar bills, must be delivered with all the related unpaid coupons—the interest payments—attached to them in order to be in good form.

Registered bonds, which *are* registered to particular individuals, must have par values in multiples of $1,000, not to exceed $100,000, in order to be delivered in good form.

Good Delivery Requirements for Stock

To be delivered in good form, stock certificates are required to be denominated in ways relating to a **round lot**, that is, 100 shares. The certificates must be denominated in multiples of 100 shares (100, 200, 300, etc.), divisors of 100 shares (100, 50, 25, 20, 10, 5, etc.), or units adding up to 100 shares (30+70, 37+59+4, etc.).

Trades of fewer than 100 shares are termed **odd lot trades**, and discrete components of trades which are fewer than 100 shares can be termed **odd lot portions**. These are not required to meet this particular good delivery requirement.

For example, in a trade of 430 shares, if the trade were comprised of two 200-share certificates and a 30-share certificate, the trade would be in good delivery form, since the two 200-share certificates would be multiples of 100, and since the 30-share certificate would be exempt as an odd lot portion. However, if the trade were comprised of one 300-share certificate and two 65-share certificates, then it would not be in good form, since, while the 300-share certificate is valid as a multiple of 100 shares, the two 65-share certificates do not meet any of the requirements and are not exempt as an odd lot portion.

Corporate Actions

Types of Corporate Actions

Splits, Reverse Splits, Spin-Offs, and Tender Offers

A stock split is an action in which existing shares of a company's stock are split into multiple shares. For instance, in a "two for one split," an owner that previously owned 100 shares will own 200 after the split. The total dollar value of the shares remains unchanged, however, as the per share value is decreased accordingly.

A reverse split is similar to a stock split, only instead of the existing shares being split into multiple shares, existing shares are combined to create fewer shares. Like a stock split, the total dollar value of shares remains unchanged, as the per share value is increased accordingly.

New independent companies can be created through spin-offs. A spinoff company is created by the sale or distribution of new shares for a division of a parent company. A business may spinoff a company in an effort to streamline their operations.

A tender offer is an offer to purchase a portion or all of the shares of a company from its shareholders.

Rights Offerings

In a **rights offering** (also called a *rights issue*), a company will issue the right to purchase additional shares, known as subscription warrants, to current shareholders in the company. The company will set a predetermined number of shares and price per share, giving shareholders the right, but not the obligation, to purchase such shares in the future, sometimes within a set time period—usually 16 to 30 days.

Since rights offerings can give an incentive for shareholders to purchase further stock, they are often used as a means to raise capital for the company. Each share's subscription price is discounted according to the market price. Rights are transferable, meaning they can be sold on the open market.

Business Combinations

A business combination is any consolidation of multiple businesses into one. There are three different kinds of business combination:

- Statutory mergers, where one company purchases all of another company's assets, leaving only the purchasing company to remain
- Statutory consolidation, where two or more companies unite to form a new company which is itself a different existing entity from the previously-existing companies
- Stock acquisition, where one company purchases the majority of another company's stock, but both companies continue as economic entities

Impact of Stock Splits and Reverse Stock Splits on Market Price and Cost Basis

The most common split is the *forward split*, which increases the number of shares outstanding, with a corresponding adjustment in share value. For example, in a 2-for-1 forward split (the most common type of split), a shareholder will receive two shares for every one they own, and the price of each new share will be half that of the former share price. Forward splits are done in most cases because a stock price has gotten so high that the cost of trading the stock has become prohibitive. More investors will be willing to buy the stock at a lower price. Forward splits are usually considered a sign of confidence on the part of the company, and it is not uncommon for share prices to rise after a forward split occurs.

A *reverse split* is the opposite—the number of shares outstanding is reduced in order to raise the price of each share, so a person who owned two shares before now owns one (in a 1-for-2 split). Reverse splits are usually considered negatively, and it is common for the price of a stock to drop after one takes place.

Adjustments to Securities Subject to Corporate Actions

In some cases, a corporate action may require an adjustment to the securities. For instance, in the case of a 2-for-1 stock split, subsequent to the corporate action (the split), adjustments could include: twice the number of shares outstanding after the split compared with prior to the split, the par value of each share is now half the amount that it was prior to the split, and the price or value of each share is half of what it was prior to the split.

Delivery of Notices and Corporate Action Deadlines

The requirement for notices and any associated deadlines will depend on how the security is traded. If the security is traded on a public exchange, then the exchange has the authority to require a notice and establish a deadline. For securities traded on OTC markets, FINRA establishes policies for notices and related deadlines.

Proxies and Proxy Voting

A stockholder has the right to vote on corporate policy and the board of directors. This vote can be cast in-person at the meeting, or by proxy, that is, by mailing-in their votes.

A voting trust is used to convey voting rights to a trustee for a specific period of time. A voting trust certificate is issued by a voting trust and given in exchange for stock. The voting trust certificate represents all the rights of stock ownership, except for the right to vote.

Non-voting common stock is similar to common stock in all ways, except it does not carry the right to vote.

The number of votes a shareholder gets corresponds to the number of shares owned. Statutory, or straight voting, is the most common form of voting. In statutory voting, each shareholder gets to cast one vote per share owned. In cumulative voting, a way of voting to elect the board of directors, each shareholder gets 1 vote per share owned multiplied by the number of directors to be elected. Contingent voting rights are voting rights given to a shareholder than are ordinarily not given, based on a specific event happening, such as when a corporation does not deliver on a promise to pay dividends to preferred stockholders.

Customer Accounts and Compliance Considerations

Account Types and Characteristics

In order to open a **new account** for a customer, a broker will need to get the customer's full legal name and date of birth, address and phone number or phone numbers, Social Security number, occupation and employer, citizenship status, annual income, and net worth. In addition, the broker must get the customer's banking and investment references, identify what investment experience and objectives the customer has, and learn whether or not the customer is an employee of another brokerage firm. Finally, the broker must also get the names and occupations of all parties authorized to make trades in the account.

- **Cash accounts** are ordinary brokerage accounts where the customer deposits cash to purchase various securities. Regulation T requires that customers with cash accounts pay for their securities within two days of having bought them.
- **Margin accounts** are brokerage accounts where, instead of paying his/her own cash, the customer is lent cash from the broker, with various securities and cash being used as collateral. The amount of cash that a customer has, plus what their broker is willing to lend them, is called their *purchasing or buying power*.
- **Options accounts** are brokerage accounts where the customer can trade various options, which are generally riskier than ordinary stocks or bonds.
- **Retirement accounts** are brokerage accounts aimed for the purposes of providing retirement income.
- **Day trading accounts** are brokerage accounts opened specifically for the purposes of trading various financial instruments within the same day, depending upon speculation for one's profits.
- **Prime brokerage accounts** are brokerage accounts where special customers receive a special set of services. These services can include cash management and securities lending, as well as mutual funds.
- **Delivery Versus Payment (DVP) accounts** involve a procedure where a security buyer's payment is due at the time of delivery.
- **Receive Versus Payment (RVP) accounts** involve a procedure where a security buyer's payment is due at the time of receipt.
- **Advisory accounts** are brokerage accounts where the customer works closely with a financial advisor but retains the final say over investment decisions.
- **Fee-based accounts** are brokerage accounts where a customer's financial advisor is compensated as a percentage of the client's assets rather than according to commissions.
- **Discretionary accounts** are accounts where brokers have the authority to engage in securities transactions apart from the client's consent. These accounts require the client and broker to sign a discretionary disclosure. (These are also called managed accounts.)

Customer Account Registrations

Individual, Joint, Corporate/Institutional, Trust, Partnerships

Brokers can register accounts for many kinds of different customers, including individuals and institutions. Some of these accounts can also be **joint accounts**, that is, accounts which are shared by two or more people. These are most likely created for people who have good grounds to trust one another, such as relatives or business partners.

One kind of joint account is **Joint Tenants with Rights of Survivorship (JTWROS)**, in which all the individuals for the account have equal authority over the account's assets, retaining control even if other joint tenants die. This kind of account differs from **Joint Tenants in Common (JTIC),** where the different individuals do *not* retain any rights of survivorship over the account. In JTIC accounts, survivors do not necessarily acquire the control over assets which were previously held by a tenant who has died. Instead, each tenant gets to distribute the assets as they desire through their will.

Brokers can register accounts for a number of different businesses, not simply individuals. They can register accounts for **sole proprietorships** (individually-owned businesses), **partnerships** (businesses owned by two or more individuals who manage and operate it), and **corporations** (a business legally separate from its owners).

Furthermore, brokers can open accounts for **unincorporated associations**, which are voluntary unions of individuals for some common purpose, generally non-profit ones. They can also open accounts for **marital property** (or community property), where property acquired by either spouse is owned by the author as well, and **trust accounts**, where a trustee manages an account for the sake of another.

Custodial

Brokers can register **custodial accounts**, which are accounts managed by an adult for the sake of minor (under 18 or 21 years old, depending on the relevant state's legislation), and are therefore a type of trust account. These accounts can be either UGMA or UTMA accounts, depending on the legislation in the state governing such an account—the **Uniform Gifts to Minors Act** or the **Uniform Transfers to Minors Act**. UGMA accounts are extensions of UTMA accounts, since they allow the transferal of gifts (including art, real estate, royalties, and intangible assets) as well as securities and cash.

Numbered accounts are accounts where the account holder's name is kept confidential, identified by a number or some code word.

Transfer on death (TOD) accounts provide the account holder with a means of easily passing on their assets to others without the various hassles and delays of probate. They simply specify which assets go to which persons.

Estate accounts are accounts held in the name of the estate of some deceased person, handled by his representative.

The **Uniform Gift to Minors Act (UGMA)** governs fiduciary accounts set up for minors (that is, accounts handled by a custodian for the sake of the minor). Anyone may donate either cash or securities to a UGMA account. Once they have, the gift may not be revoked or returned. The account administrator, or custodian, trades on behalf of the minor, and may use proceeds of the account to pay for the minor's living expenses, education, etc., when appropriate. The minor has no control of the funds until reaching adulthood, at which point the account becomes theirs to manage.

Only one minor and one custodian can be on each account, although a minor can be the beneficial owner of more than one account, and a custodian can manage more than one account.

Uniform Transfer to Minors Act (UTMA) accounts are very similar to UGMA accounts. However, the main difference is that they permit gifts besides cash and securities, e.g., land, intangible assets (like patents), art, etc.

Margin activity is prohibited to UGMA and UTMA accounts; they must be **cash accounts only**. The custodian is not allowed to use the assets of the account as collateral on a loan. Any cash coming into the account, along with interest and dividends, must be put to use by investing it within a reasonable time period. Except for covered calls, where the underlying stock is already owned, options trading and commodities trading are off limits to UGMA accounts. The custodian is not allowed to borrow money from the account, although the custodian can make loans to the account. All investments are expected to be prudent and have the minor's best interests at heart.

Retirement

Individual Retirement Arrangements (IRAs)

Although the IRS definition of the acronym IRA is individual retirement arrangement, they are most commonly referred to as individual retirement accounts. IRAs were created by federal legislation to provide an immediate benefit and thereby encourage individuals to save for retirement. Nearly all people with earned income in a year may contribute to an IRA in that same year. IRAs are considered qualified accounts; that is, they meet IRS stipulations regarding tax-deductible contributions and tax-deferred growth. There are three types of individual retirement accounts available to investors. Each has different rules and regulations regarding taxation, eligible contributions and limits to those contributions, and characteristics of distributions from the accounts. The three types of IRAs are traditional IRAs, Roth IRAs, and simplified employee pension plans, or SEP IRAs. Although they receive similar tax treatment, IRAs are not the same thing as 401(k)s, 403(b)s, etc.

Contributions and Distributions

Traditional IRAs are accounts to which investors may contribute up to $6,500 ($7,500 if that person is over fifty years of age) per year, per individual (2023). The money contributed to the account must be earned income; that is, wages, salaries, and tips, commissions and bonuses, self-employment income, alimony, and nontaxable combat income. If the investor's total earned income is less than $6,000, the amount of the contribution is limited to the amount of earned income. Unearned income includes, but is not necessarily limited to, capital gains, interest and dividend income, income received from pensions and annuities, child support, and passive income from other investments held. Phase-out income limitations (as measured by adjusted gross income) apply to the tax-benefitted nature of IRAs. Investors may not withdraw funds from the account without incurring a 10% penalty in addition to ordinary income tax on the withdrawal, unless the IRS deems the withdrawal to be for an extenuating circumstance. After the investor reaches the age of 72, they must begin taking regular distributions called **required minimum distributions**, or RMDs.

Roth IRAs

Roth IRAs are a modification of traditional IRAs that originated with the Taxpayer Relief Act of 1997. Unlike contributions to traditional IRAs, Roth IRA contributions are not tax deductible. This feature, however, results in tax-free distributions that include the growth in the account. The limit of contributions per year to Roth IRAs is $6,500 of earned income, or $7,500 if the investor is over fifty (2023). The extra $1,000 "catch-up" contribution for investors over fifty is a result of the Economic Growth and Tax Relief Reconciliation Act of 2001, or EGTRRA. Individuals who file single income tax returns may not contribute to Roth IRAs if they made over $144,000 in 2022. Married couples filing jointly may not contribute if their combined income is over $214,000 in 2022. Distributions from Roth IRA accounts vary from other retirement accounts. Since the contributions have already been taxed, the investor may continue to contribute to a Roth IRA indefinitely and is not required to take minimum distributions as is required with other retirement accounts.

Conversions, Rollovers, and Early Withdrawal

When an investor converts a traditional IRA to a Roth IRA, the investor will pay income tax on the amount converted, including both tax-deductible contributions and tax-deferred earnings that have accrued. The benefit of a conversion is that the investor will not be required to pay income tax on any funds when they are withdrawn from the Roth IRA.

A rollover occurs when the assets of one retirement plan are transferred to another retirement plan. A direct rollover occurs when the assets are transferred directly from one plan to another. An indirect rollover occurs when the assets are paid to the investor and then the investor transfers the assets to another plan. Rollovers do not incur a tax liability as long as the funds are transferred into the destination plan within 60 days of leaving the original plan. Funds can only be rolled over into a retirement account of the same tax status. For example, funds cannot be directly rolled over from a tax-deferred 401k into a Roth IRA; they would have to be first rolled over to a traditional IRA and then converted to a Roth IRA.

Funds that are withdrawn from a retirement account before the account owner reaches the age of 59½ are subject to an additional 10% federal income tax penalty. However, the penalty is waived if the funds are used to pay for unreimbursed medical expenses, to pay for health insurance premiums while unemployed, or to pay for higher education expenses.

401(K) PLANS

A 401(k) plan is a qualified retirement plan to which employees may contribute a percentage of their salary through payroll deductions. The maximum salary deferral in this method is $22,500 (as of 2023), and the max annual additions (elective deferrals, employer matches, employer nonelective contributions, allocations of forfeitures) is the lesser of 100% of the participants compensation or $56,000. Contributions to a 401(k) plan are made with pretax dollars, which has the effect of lowering the investor's overall tax obligation for the year. While this amount will be deducted from earnings for federal income tax, such contributions do not lower the salary amount on which FICA is based. Generally, investors may not make withdrawals from 401(k) accounts prior to age 59½. There are, however, what the IRS considers hardship withdrawals from 401(k) plans that usually allow the investor to avoid the 10% penalty, even though they will still be required to pay their regular income tax rate on the withdrawal.

ROTH 401(K) PLANS

A Roth 401(k) plan mixes the features of Roth IRAs with those of 401(k) plans. Like Roth IRAs, Roth 401(k) plans are funded with after-tax dollars. This allows the account to grow tax free and distributions to be made tax free. Employers are not allowed to contribute to Roth 401(k) plans on the employee's behalf. Therefore, two 401(k) plans must be maintained simultaneously: a regular 401(k) to which the employer may contribute, and the Roth 401(k). An advantage of the Roth 401(k) over the Roth IRA is that there is no income limit for an investor to be able to contribute to a Roth 401(k). Investors may contribute up to $20,500 to Roth 401(k) plans (2022). The distributions from Roth 401(k) plans are not taxable, but distributions from the employer-funded plan would be. Unlike Roth IRAs, the investor must start taking distributions from Roth 401(k) plans by age 70½.

403(B) PLANS

A 403(b) retirement account is a deferred taxation plan similar to a 401(k) plan. They are reserved for tax-exempt organizations, whereas 401(k) plans are used by for-profit companies. Such tax-exempt organizations include, but are not limited to, churches, schools, and hospitals. Occasionally, 403(b) plans are referred to as tax-sheltered annuities. The maximum amount of annual salary deferral is $20,500 (as of 2022). Contributions to a 403(b) plan are made with pretax dollars, which has the effect of lowering the investor's overall tax obligation. While this amount will be deducted from the investor's earnings for federal income tax, the contributions do not lower the salary on which FICA is based. Generally, investors may not make withdrawals from 403(b) accounts prior to age 59½. There are, however, what the IRS considers hardship withdrawals from 403(b) plans that usually allow investors to avoid the 10% penalty, even though they will still be required to pay regular income tax rate on the withdrawal.

Section 457 Plans

A Section 457 plan is a retirement plan that falls under the deferred compensation designation. They are so-called because they are established under section 457 of the Internal Revenue Code. A 457 plan is set up for the benefit of employees of a state, political subdivision thereof, or any agency of the state. They may also be used for employees of certain tax-exempt organizations, except churches, and then only for highly paid employees. Special rules regarding 457 plans are that they are exempt from ERISA and they are not subject to non-discrimination rules. Nongovernmental employees may not roll 457 plans into IRAs, but there is no early withdrawal penalty for withdrawal before age 59½. A 457 plan may be concurrently funded with 403(b) plans without the contribution limits of one plan affecting the other. Also, of note is that loans may not be taken against a 457 plan, unlike a 401(k) plan.

Nonqualified Retirement Plans

Nonqualified retirement plans differ from retirement plans in that the contributions are not tax deductible to the employer, although some types of nonqualified plans grow tax deferred. The employer instead benefits from a tax break when money is distributed from the account. Employers benefit from these types of retirement plans because they are not subject to the same types of rules as qualified plans. The employer may discriminate as to the employees who benefit from this type of plan. This is particularly useful when rewarding a key employee but not sharing the benefit with other less-essential personnel. Nonqualified plans are exempt from the reporting and disclosure requirements of qualified plans. Despite this exemption, though, the plan must be in writing and effectively communicated to the participants.

Anti-Money Laundering (AML)

Definition of Money Laundering

Money laundering is a process by which money received illegally is given legitimacy through a legal paper trail. It is called money laundering because illegally obtained funds (dirty money) are given a legal or clean appearance (laundered). The Bank Secrecy Act (BSA) requires that all broker-dealers develop anti-money laundering programs to help combat the crime.

Stages of Money Laundering

There are three fundamental steps that money launderers follow. The first step is **placement** into the monetary system. This is typically the stage when it is easiest to catch. One strategy that is frequently employed in this stage is called **structuring** or smurfing. Financial institutions must file a currency transaction report for any cash transactions exceeding $10,000, so the money launderer makes multiple smaller deposits to avoid showing up on the transaction report. If an individual or business makes *frequent* cash deposits that are slightly less than $10,000, this would be a red flag.

The second step in the money laundering process is **layering**. In this step, the money launderers are attempting to obscure the source of the funds by transacting multiple times. These transactions can vary in many ways and help the criminal throw off investigators by varying the amounts and frequency so that they do not coincide with the crimes.

Integration is the last step of money laundering. The illegal funds are intermingled with legitimate money, often by associating the illegal funds with legal funds of an actual business. This often makes the laundered funds indistinguishable from legitimate money.

AML Compliance Program

Money laundering is the deliberate concealment of the source of illegally-obtained funds, and due to its deception and harm, a number of regulations and procedures exist for anti-money laundering compliance. Each company or firm should individually assess their specific risks in order to create a compliance program that best suits their business and mitigates the identified risks.

Suspicious Activity Report (SAR)

Suspicious activity reports (SARs) are made by financial institutions to the U.S. Treasury Department (specifically, the Financial Crimes Enforcement Network, or FinCEN), detailing information about suspicious individuals or transactions.

The **Bank Secrecy Act** (BSA), passed in 1970, established responsibilities for financial institutions to federal government agencies, requiring the institutions to maintain records for cash purchases of negotiable instruments, to file any such purchases totaling over $10,000, and to report any suspicious activity.

Currency Transaction Report (CTR)

Currency transaction reports (CTRs) must be filed by financial institutions to the federal government for any currency transaction exceeding $10,000. Before 1986, out of regard for financial privacy, these were not required.

FinCEN

FinCEN refers to the Financial Crimes Enforcement Network of the U.S. Department of the Treasury. Their goal is to protect the banking system from illegal activities, promote secure financial transactions, and utilize data analytics to support their mission.

Office of Foreign Asset Control (OFAC) and the Specially Designated Nationals and Blocked Persons (SDNs) List

The Office of Foreign Asset Control (OFAC) is a section of the U.S. Treasury Department tasked with the objective of national security over foreign policy goals through economic and trade sanctions, as well as the tracking of terrorist activity. Their relevance to anti-money laundering compliance is to discover any financial activity involving the financing of terrorism. The OFAC has compiled a list of Specially Designated Nationals (SDNs), that is, people or groups of people with whom U.S. citizens and institutions are prohibited from doing business.

Books and Records and Privacy Requirements

Books and Records Retention Requirements

One of the duties of a broker for his customers is to retain various **books and records**. According to **MSRB Rule G-8**, these include records of original entry, account records, securities records, and subsidiary records, such as records for municipal securities in transfer, municipal securities to be validated, municipal securities borrowed or loaned, and municipal securities transactions not completed on the settlement date. The broker should also maintain records for put options and repurchase agreements, records for agency transactions, records for transactions as principal, records concerning primary offerings, and other records. Essentially, the broker should maintain a paper trail for all of his customer's substantial activity.

Confirmations and Account Statements

FINRA Rule 2340 states that, in most cases, firms should send customers an account statement at least every quarter, including relevant balances, activity, and positions. If the account has activity, then the customer will usually receive a monthly statement of all transactions. The statement should include instructions to the customer if the customer feels that something on the statement is erroneous or they do not understand their statement. Firms should maintain customer account statements for six years.

Holding of Customer Mail

A firm should only hold a customer's mail if the customer has sent written instructions requesting that the firm hold the mail for a specified period of time because the customer will be unable to retrieve their mail from the usual mail delivery location.

Business Continuity Plans (BCP)

Though the two terms can be distinguished, **business continuity and disaster recovery (BC/DR) planning** is generally considered as one process by which a firm, in this case a broker-dealer, takes actions to resume the firm's ordinary operations in the case of a significant disrupting event. Plans for these kinds of situation must be in writing, approved by a principal, and include several preventative measures, such as the availability of backup data, alternative communication for a firm with its regulators, customers, and employees, a backup location for employees to work, and a means by which to give customers access to their securities in case of a disaster. Firms must conduct an annual review of their business continuity plan to determine whether any modifications are necessary in light of changes to the member's operations, structure, business, or location.

Customer Protection and Custody of Assets

Broker-dealers are obligated to ensure that their customers' funds and securities are held in a secure fashion. This includes all securities over which the firm has custody or control, without exception. Segregation describes the process of separating the firm's securities from their customers' securities. Occasionally, a customer will request that a security be registered "in street name" meaning that the security is registered to the broker-dealer but in fact belongs to the customer. Securities held in street name and securities that belong to the broker-dealer must be segregated from securities that are registered to the customer. Margined securities, however, that are used to collateralize margin accounts do not have to be segregated from broker-dealer securities.

When a carrying firm is said to have custody or possession of funds and/or securities, those funds and/or securities are held "in-house" at the firm. Custodied funds have been completely purchased by the customer, and they do not owe the firm any more money for them. Funds/securities over which a broker-dealer has transactional authority but does not hold them are considered controlled funds, as the broker-dealer exerts control over the account on the customer's behalf. After the firm that custodies the funds completes all of their settlement records, there are policies and procedures in place to guarantee that the firm has taken physical custody or control over all of their customers' securities.

Privacy Requirements

Regulation S-P (Privacy of Consumer Financial Information) contains at its core three main purposes or functions:

1. The regulation requires financial institutions to notify its customers of its privacy practices;
2. The regulation prohibits financial institutions from disclosing nonpublic personal customer information to third parties, unless the institution has disclosed its practices to the customer and the customer has failed to opt out of such disclosure; and
3. The regulation provides certain industry standards for financial institutions regarding privacy practices and disclosure of customer information.

Through the various components of Regulation S-P, customers of financial institutions are afforded additional protection from the distribution of their personal information, while financial institutions are provided with a "road map" to follow to ensure they are staying in compliance with the regulation.

Disclosure Limitations in Regulation S-P

Regulation S-P (Privacy of Consumer Financial Information) provides for a number of improvements to the required **disclosure** by financial institutions to their customers regarding the institutions privacy practices and providing of personal customer information to third parties. For example, financial institutions regulated under Regulation S-P must provide disclosure to customers including the nonpublic personal data that is collected, how that data is used, and with whom it can be shared. Additionally, the financial institution must provide the opportunity for its customers to "opt-out," which means that they can choose to prohibit the financial institution from sharing this information with third parties. As technology has become an increasingly important component of the financial markets, so too has the concern over privacy laws, identity theft, and the protection of personal information. This is an issue that will continue to play an important role in consumer protection in the years to come.

Exceptions to Regulation S-P

Regulation S-P (Privacy of Consumer Financial Information) provides for certain **exceptions to the disclosure and privacy policies**. A good working knowledge of these exceptions is important to avoid confusion or miscommunication around practices that might otherwise be considered violations of the regulation. For instance, the regulation provides that the initial privacy notice must be provided at the beginning of the customer relationship, which is defined to occur at the time of share purchases. However, this privacy delivery requirement may be delayed if:

1. Providing the notice prior to the customer relationship would delay the customer's transaction and the customer agrees to receive the notice at a later date; or
2. A nonaffiliated broker or dealer creates the customer relationship with the fund without the fund's prior knowledge.

Additionally, there are exceptions to the ability of the customer to opt-out of the sharing of personal nonpublic information, when the institution must share that information with a third party in order to effect transactions on behalf of the customer or servicing a customer's products and accounts.

Communications with the Public and General Suitability Requirements

Communication with the Public and Telemarketing

Cold calling is an interaction with a potential customer, usually by telephone, for which the customer had no previous anticipation. ("Warm calling" occurs after a customer has expressed some interest in an investment product.)

FINRA has various rules governing cold calling, including a prohibition of calls before **8 A.M. and after 9 P.M.** and a prohibition of cold-calling those who have placed themselves on the **do-not-call list** (either for specific firms or for the national list, kept by the Federal Trade Commission).

While cold calling is forbidden in the above situations, that does not mean that all phone solicitations are so forbidden. The time-of-day restraint is not applicable, for example, to those with whom one has established a business relationship or to those who have invited or permitted one to call. Similarly, people listed on do-not-call registries can still be called, without any rules being violated, if there is a personal relationship, established business relationship, or prior express written consent.

Suitability Requirements

The USA PATRIOT Act was initiated to help the government and financial institutions identify potential terrorist funding operations. The **Customer Information Program (CIP)** was established to aid financial institutions in gathering the required information. To comply with CIP, the institution must obtain the client's name, date of birth, physical address, and social security number. The CIP program is integral to the **"know your customer" (KYC)** controls. To meet KYC standards, the institution should start with gathering CIP information, run the client's name against lists of currently sought-after parties, determine the risk associated with the customer and potential money laundering and other illegal activities, establish a normal pattern of behavior for the customer, and monitor their transactions to ensure that their behavior does not deviate from their normal patterns.

Corporate insiders are individuals who are particularly privy to a corporation's "**inside**" information; this definition includes directors and officers for the company in addition to anyone owning over 10% of the voting shares, and really anyone who has access to **material but non-public knowledge**. These insiders have an extra set of restrictions for any securities transactions they wish to make, and brokers should consider them accordingly.

Another consideration which brokers have to make is whether their clients are employees of a broker-dealer. Just as corporate insiders are subject to various trading restrictions based upon their inside knowledge, so also employees of broker-dealers (especially of competing broker-dealers) carry their own set of risks. Particularly, the broker's company must receive consent from the employee's own institution.

Employees of self-regulatory organizations (SROs) likewise are subject to these restrictions. As with employees of other broker-dealers, brokers are required to obtain the consent of a client's institution if he is employed for an SRO.

The term **suitability**, as it applies to investing, refers to the act of determining the client's **needs** and applying those needs in the consideration of securities best suited to those needs. Clients in need of current income and capital preservation will not benefit from the purchase of common stock of risky companies with small-market capitalization (small cap). The common stock of small-cap companies does not typically pay dividends, resulting in no income, and they are volatile, working against the need of capital preservation. Conversely, a young investor whose goal is capital appreciation and has the ability to absorb and recover from losses would not be suited to fixed income securities. The younger investor has no need of income from his or her investments, and the stability of the investments detracts from the goal of capital appreciation. Common stock of small-cap companies is more suited to the younger investor's needs. The investor's risk appetite should also be considered when determining suitability. A younger investor may not be able to accept large swings in his or her portfolio, thereby requiring a more conservative strategy than other investors of similar demographics. Members should only provide clients with recommendations for which the investment characteristics, risks, and potential rewards match the investor's needs and objectives.

Prohibited Activities

Market Manipulation

Definition of Market Manipulation

Market manipulation refers to the manipulation of financial markets by creating **false or inflated prices** for securities. Market manipulation can be accomplished by large investors making an unusually large number of transactions below the current value of a security to purposely create fear that the asset is underperforming and drive down the prices. Alternatively, those who engage in market manipulation may create multiple buy and sell orders for a single security, artificially inflating the volume of trading for the security. Both of these practices can lead to other events that may change the direction of markets to the benefit of those practicing market manipulation. Market manipulation is illegal in the United States and is an unethical practice.

Types of Market Manipulation

A few kinds of prohibited market manipulation include:

- **Pumping and dumping** refers to bloating the market price of a security that one owns, often through confident recommendations grounded in deceptive assertions, and then selling it before the bubble pops and the price decreases back to a more reasonable valuation.
- **Marking the close** refers to purchasing a security at a high price minutes before trading ends for the day. This makes the security's closing price appear high on exchanges, which then deceptively influences traders at the beginning of the next day.
- **Marking the open** is the opposite, referring to transactions done very early in the trading day to manipulate other traders' perceptions.
- **Backing away** refers to proposing a large securities purchase (or sale) in order to influence trading, only to then "back away" from the transaction if a seller or buyer agrees with your offer (usually this requires a large or institutional investor).
- **Freeriding** refers to purchasing a security without having the funds to do so; the idea is that one would cover the cost of the purchase with the proceeds of a subsequent sale.

Brokers are legally prohibited from engaging in a number of behaviors designed to unduly benefit themselves or hurt others.

- They are not permitted to **spread market rumors** in order to influence other people to buy or sell a security. This is because market transactions ought to be based on real facts and knowledge.
- They are not permitted to engage in **front running**, which is when a broker makes a trade due to their foreknowledge of a block trade (a trade of 10,000+ stocks) before it is reported.
- They are not permitted to engage in **churning**, which occurs when a broker participates in excessive trading on a client's behalf only to obtain extra commissions.
- They are not permitted to engage in **commingling**, which is the combination of a customer's fully-paid securities and their margined securities, or the combination of a customer's securities with a firm's securities.
- They are not permitted to **prearrange trades**, which would be an agreement between a broker and a customer to buy back some security at a given price.
- They are not permitted to **guarantee against losses**, since that would be frankly misrepresenting the riskiness of investments.

- They are not permitted to **pay for referrals** by compensating others (whether with cash or something else) for finding, introducing, or referring a client.
- They are not permitted to make **unsuitable recommendations**, which is simply to say that they ought to recommend good investments. If this is serious enough, customers can sue brokers for failing in their obligations.

INSIDER TRADING

DEFINITION OF INSIDER TRADING

The term "insider trading" refers to an individual with "inside" knowledge of a publicly traded company capitalizing on the knowledge to make money. The only instance in which this is legal is when the knowledge that the insider has is publicly available. The term "insider" generally refers to officers, directors, and board members of publicly traded companies, but the term may be applied to any person who may be privy to non-public information, such as the spouse of a director, or a custodial employee who has overheard the non-public information. Depending on the severity of the insider-trading charge, a conviction of insider trading can carry felony prison terms for perpetrators. Additionally, inside traders can be compelled to pay up to three times the amount of money made or three times the amount of loss avoided associated with their inside trading transaction.

DEFINITION OF MATERIAL NONPUBLIC INFORMATION

The Insider Trading and Securities Fraud Enforcement Act of 1988 was created to establish clear definitions of "non-public material information" and "insiders." In order to be guilty of insider trading a person must have acted on non-public material information. The act defines non-public material information as information that is not known outside of a specific company.

IDENTIFYING INVOLVED PARTIES

An insider is any person who acts as an officer or director of a company or a shareholder with over 10%. The definition of insider also extends to anyone holding non-public material information, such as accounting and finance staff, and their direct family including spouses. The act is a federal legislation that was created to eliminate the occurrence of insider trading and securities fraud. As a means of enforcement, the act designates specific penalties for violators. Violators can be fined, sued or criminally prosecuted.

PENALTIES

The Insider Trading and Securities Fraud Enforcement Act of 1988 imposed new and more stringent civil and criminal penalties for those who have violated insider trading laws. Under the Act, the SEC was granted the authority to impose **damages** for three times the amount of profit gained or loss avoided in the illegal transactions up to a maximum of $1,000,000. The **criminal penalties** for violating insider trading laws were made more stringent by the Act. The maximum **fines** were increased from $100,000 to $1,000,000 for individuals and from $500,000 to $2,500,000 for non-natural persons. Additionally, the maximum **jail sentence** was increased from five years to 10 years. Finally, the Act provides that all non-natural persons are subject to the higher fines under the criminal penalties as compared to the civil penalties.

OTHER PROHIBITED ACTIVITIES

RESTRICTIONS PREVENTING ASSOCIATED PERSONS FROM PURCHASING INITIAL PUBLIC OFFERINGS (IPO)

The Financial Industry Regulatory Authority (FINRA) expressly forbids broker-dealers registered with FINRA from selling shares of initial public offerings (IPOs) to restricted persons, or to accounts in which restricted persons have a significant interest. This rule is in place to protect customers that may wish to participate in the IPO but are unable to do so because the restricted persons have had unfair access to the IPO shares. Persons considered restricted for this purpose are FINRA member firms, a party owning more than 9% of a FINRA member firm, financial consultants and/or accountants, employees of FINRA member firms, representatives of the firm that is underwriting the issue, and portfolio managers. Also included in the definition of restricted person is any immediate family member of any of the above-mentioned parties. Extended family members that reside with restricted persons are also considered restricted.

Use of Manipulative, Deceptive or Other Fraudulent Devices

FINRA Rule 2020, Use of Manipulative, Deceptive or Other Fraudulent Devices, states: "No member shall effect any transaction in, or induce the purchase or sale of, any security by means of any manipulative, deceptive, or other fraudulent device or contrivance." The importance of this rule is in ensuring the integrity of the capital markets and the confidence of retail investors that the markets are not "rigged" for the larger, institutional investors or those with critical inside information. A member would be in violation of Rule 2020 if they used falsified, enhanced financial reports to entice an investor to purchase a certain security. In addition to being dishonest and illegal, such activities have significant negative repercussions for the markets as they reduce market efficiency and drastically reduce market participation among smaller investors if discovered.

Improper Use of Customers' Securities or Funds

The Uniform Securities Act has specific provisions that place limits on a security professional's ability to **borrow from clients**. As a general rule, securities professionals are prohibited from borrowing either securities or funds from their clients. This behavior is considered unethical and is a violation of the Uniform Securities Act. However, there are limited circumstances in which such behavior is permissible. If the client is a lending institution such as a bank or saving and loan that lends money as a standard business offering, the securities professional may borrow money from its client.

Similarly, if the client is a securities firm or other business that offers securities loans as a standard business offering, the securities professional may borrow securities from the client as a customer of that client.

As a general rule, agents cannot **share a client's profits or losses**; however, there are certain circumstances where this is permitted. If an agent obtains prior approval from a client in writing and shares ownership of an account with a client, the agent may share profits and losses associated with the joint account with the client. In this situation, profits and losses for the joint account are shared based on the percentage of account owned by each party. For example, if the agent owns fifteen percent of the account and the client owns eighty-five percent of the account, the account's profits and loss will be split according to these percentages.

Although **agents** are permitted to have joint accounts with their clients under the circumstances described above, broker-dealers are not. **Broker-dealers** are prohibited from establishing joint accounts with their clients.

Financial Exploitation of Seniors

FINRA directs investment firms to specifically consider the age and life circumstances (e.g., whether retired or not) of senior clients and take precautions with regard to investment recommendations and sales practices towards this demographic. FINRA also created two rules designed to address senior financial exploitation. FINRA Rule 4512 requires a member to duly try to acquire contact info for a "trusted contact person," who could then be contacted and trusted to administer an exploited person's account in the event of their exploitation. FINRA Rule 2165 allows a member, if they have reasonable grounds for believing exploitation has occurred, to temporarily place a hold on any disbursement of funds or securities from the exploited person's account. This latter rule applies not only to seniors (defined as those age 65 and older) but also to mentally or physically impaired adults (age 18 or older).

Activities of Unregistered Persons

Only persons registered with FINRA may accept payment and commissions for sales of securities executed (excluding trading exempt securities). There are instances in which persons may wish to pay commissions to an unregistered person; this should be avoided at all times. Such situations may include a bank teller sending a high net-worth individual to a registered person, and the representative giving the teller money as an incentive and a thank-you. As innocuous as a situation like this may seem, it is not allowed under FINRA regulations.

Providing a non-FINRA member with a member discount may also be construed as a commission. This is allowable only if the person discounted is associated with a FINRA member. For these purposes, members of FINRA that have been suspended or barred are not considered members. Similarly, unregistered persons are prohibited from soliciting customers and taking orders from them. FINRA requires all these transactional activities to be done solely by registered persons.

Falsifying or Withholding Documents

The Financial Industry Regulatory Authority (FINRA) expressly forbids the falsification of client documents such as statements and confirmations. Statements are particularly easy to falsify, since there is not an industry standard and each FINRA member creates their own. Members may attempt to allay customers' fears and keep their business by inflating their securities prices on the statement or on confirmations sent to the customer. This is in no case legal or ethical. Neither is it legal or ethical to withhold the statements or confirmation beyond the accepted time periods, such as trade settlement dates for confirmations. The only case in which holding documents is acceptable is in the event the customer supplies a written request to withhold these documents for up to two months if they're traveling within the United States or three months if traveling outside the United States.

Prohibited Activities Related to Maintenance of Books and Records

Firms are obligated to protect the integrity of their books and records; therefore, brokers are prohibited from engaging in any activities that might compromise the integrity or confidentiality of such records. Additionally, each firm should establish a standard policy for the retention of records. Their policy should adhere to all requirements of the SEC and FINRA. Firms are not permitted to falsify records in any way, improperly dispose of records, or violate record retention standards.

Additional Rules and Regulations

In addition to the content included in this chapter, those sitting for the SIE Exam will need to be familiar with the following rules and regulations:

FINRA Rules

- 2010 – Standards of Commercial Honor and Principles of Trade
  https://www.finra.org/rules-guidance/rulebooks/finra-rules/2010
- 2020 – Use of Manipulative, Deceptive or Other Fraudulent Devices
  https://www.finra.org/rules-guidance/rulebooks/finra-rules/2020
- 2040 – Payments to Unregistered Persons
  https://www.finra.org/rules-guidance/rulebooks/finra-rules/2040
- 2090 – Know Your Customer
  https://www.finra.org/rules-guidance/rulebooks/finra-rules/2090
- 2111 – Suitability
  https://www.finra.org/rules-guidance/rulebooks/finra-rules/2111
- 2120 – Commissions, Mark Ups and Charges
  https://www.finra.org/rules-guidance/rulebooks/finra-rules/2120
- 2150 – Improper Use of Customers' Securities or Funds; Prohibition Against Guarantees and Sharing in Accounts
  https://www.finra.org/rules-guidance/rulebooks/finra-rules/2150
- 2165 – Financial Exploitation of Specified Adults
  https://www.finra.org/rules-guidance/rulebooks/finra-rules/2165
- 2210 – Communications with the Public
  https://www.finra.org/rules-guidance/rulebooks/finra-rules/2210
- 2220 – Options Communications
  https://www.finra.org/rules-guidance/rulebooks/retired-rules/2220
- 2231 – Customer Account Statements
  https://www.finra.org/rules-guidance/rulebooks/finra-rules/2231
- 2251 – Forwarding of Proxy and Other Issuer-related Materials
  https://www.finra.org/rules-guidance/rulebooks/finra-rules/2251
- 2264 – Margin Disclosure Statement
  https://www.finra.org/rules-guidance/rulebooks/finra-rules/2264
- 2232 – Customer Confirmations
  https://www.finra.org/rules-guidance/rulebooks/finra-rules/2232
- 3150 – Holding of Customer Mail
  https://www.finra.org/rules-guidance/rulebooks/finra-rules/3150
- 3210 – Accounts at Other Broker-Dealers and Financial Institutions
  https://www.finra.org/rules-guidance/rulebooks/finra-rules/3210
- 3230 – Telemarketing
  https://www.finra.org/rules-guidance/rulebooks/finra-rules/3230
- 3240 – Borrowing from or Lending to Customers
  https://www.finra.org/rules-guidance/rulebooks/finra-rules/3240
- 3250 – Designation of Accounts
  https://www.finra.org/rules-guidance/rulebooks/finra-rules/3250
- 3260 – Discretionary Accounts
  https://www.finra.org/rules-guidance/rulebooks/finra-rules/3260
- 3310 – Anti-money Laundering Compliance Program
  https://www.finra.org/rules-guidance/rulebooks/finra-rules/3310

- 4210 – Margin Requirements
https://www.finra.org/rules-guidance/rulebooks/finra-rules/4210
- 4370 – Business Continuity Plans and Emergency Contact Information
https://www.finra.org/rules-guidance/rulebooks/finra-rules/4370
- 4511 – General Requirements
https://www.finra.org/rules-guidance/rulebooks/finra-rules/4511
- 4512 – Customer Account Information
https://www.finra.org/rules-guidance/rulebooks/finra-rules/4512
- 4514 – Authorization Records for Negotiable Instruments Drawn From a Customer's Account
https://www.finra.org/rules-guidance/rulebooks/finra-rules/4514
- 5130 – Restrictions on the Purchase and Sale of Initial Equity Public Offerings
https://www.finra.org/rules-guidance/rulebooks/finra-rules/5130
- 5210 – Publication of Transactions and Quotations
https://www.finra.org/rules-guidance/rulebooks/finra-rules/5210
- 5220 – Offers at Stated Prices
https://www.finra.org/rules-guidance/rulebooks/finra-rules/5220
- 5230 – Payments Involving Publications that Influence the Market Price of a Security
https://www.finra.org/rules-guidance/rulebooks/finra-rules/5230
- 5240 – Anti-intimidation/Coordination
https://www.finra.org/rules-guidance/rulebooks/finra-rules/5240
- 5270 – Front Running of Block Transactions
https://www.finra.org/rules-guidance/rulebooks/finra-rules/5270
- 5280 – Trading Ahead of Research Reports
https://www.finra.org/rules-guidance/rulebooks/finra-rules/5280
- 5290 – Order Entry and Execution Practices
https://www.finra.org/rules-guidance/rulebooks/finra-rules/5290
- 5310 – Best Execution and Interpositioning
https://www.finra.org/rules-guidance/rulebooks/finra-rules/5310
- 5320 – Prohibition Against Trading Ahead of Customer Orders
https://www.finra.org/rules-guidance/rulebooks/finra-rules/5320
- 6438 – Displaying Priced Quotations in Multiple Quotation Mediums
https://www.finra.org/rules-guidance/rulebooks/finra-rules/6438

MSRB Rules

- G-8 – Books and Records to be Made by Brokers, Dealers, Municipal Securities Dealers, and Municipal Advisors
http://www.msrb.org/Rules-and-Interpretations/MSRB-Rules/General/Rule-G-8.aspx
- G-9 – Preservation of Records
http://www.msrb.org/Rules-and-Interpretations/MSRB-Rules/General/Rule-G-9.aspx
- G-13 – Quotations
http://www.msrb.org/Rules-and-Interpretations/MSRB-Rules/General/Rule-G-13.aspx
- G-14 – Reports of Sales or Purchases
http://www.msrb.org/Rules-and-Interpretations/MSRB-Rules/General/Rule-G-14.aspx
- G-15 – Confirmation, Clearance, Settlement and Other Uniform Practice Requirements with Respect to Transactions with Customers
http://www.msrb.org/Rules-and-Interpretations/MSRB-Rules/General/Rule-G-15.aspx
- G-18 – Best Execution
http://www.msrb.org/Rules-and-Interpretations/MSRB-Rules/General/Rule-G-18.aspx

- G-21 – Advertising
  http://www.msrb.org/Rules-and-Interpretations/MSRB-Rules/General/Rule-G-21.aspx
- G-25 – Improper Use of Assets
  http://www.msrb.org/Rules-and-Interpretations/MSRB-Rules/General/Rule-G-25.aspx
- G-39 – Telemarketing
  http://www.msrb.org/Rules-and-Interpretations/MSRB-Rules/General/Rule-G-39.aspx
- G-41 – Anti-money Laundering Compliance Program
  http://www.msrb.org/Rules-and-Interpretations/MSRB-Rules/General/Rule-G-41.aspx
- G-47 – Time of Trade Disclosure
  http://www.msrb.org/Rules-and-Interpretations/MSRB-Rules/General/Rule-G-47.aspx

SEC Rules and Regulations

- Regulation M
  https://www.ecfr.gov/cgi-bin/text-idx?node=sg17.4.242.sg0
- Regulation S-P – Privacy of Consumer Financial Information and Safeguarding Personal Information
  https://www.ecfr.gov/cgi-bin/text-idx?node=pt17.4.248
- Securities Exchange Act of 1934
  http://legcounsel.house.gov/Comps/Securities%20Exchange%20Act%20Of%201934.pdf
  - Section 10 – Regulation of the Use of Manipulative and Deceptive Devices
  - Section 11(d) – Trading by Members of Exchanges, Brokers and Dealers – "Prohibition on Extension of Credit by Broker-Dealer"
  - Section 14 – Proxies
  - Section 15 – Rules Relating to Over-the-Counter Markets Section
  - 20A – Liability to Contemporaneous Traders for Insider Trading Section
  - 21A – Civil Penalties for Insider Trading
  - 10b-1 – Prohibition of Use of Manipulative or Deceptive Devices or Contrivances with Respect to Certain Securities Exempted from Registration
  - 10b-3 – Employment of Manipulative and Deceptive Devices by Brokers or Dealers
  - 10b-5 – Employment of Manipulative and Deceptive Devices
  - 10b5-1 – Trading on Material Nonpublic Information in Insider Trading Cases
  - 10b5-2 – Duties of Trust or Confidence in Misappropriation Insider Trading Cases
  - 10b-10 – Confirmation of Transactions
  - 15c1-2 – Fraud and Misrepresentation
  - 15c1-3 – Misrepresentation by Brokers, Dealers and Municipal Securities Dealers as to Registration
  - 15c2-12 – Municipal Securities Disclosure
  - 17a-3 – Records to be Made by Certain Exchange Members, Brokers and Dealers
  - 17a-4 – Records to be Preserved by Certain Exchange Members, Brokers and Dealers
- Investment Company Act of 1940
  http://legcounsel.house.gov/Comps/Investment%20Company%20Act%20Of%201940.pdf
  - 17a-6 – Exemption for Transactions with Portfolio Affiliates
  - 17a-7 – Exemption of Certain Purchase or Sale Transactions Between an Investment Company and Certain Affiliated Persons Thereof

Insider Trading & Securities Fraud Enforcement Act of 1988 (ITSFEA)

(Consisted of amendments now included in the Securities Exchange Act of 1934)

Federal Reserve Board

- Regulation T
  https://www.ecfr.gov/cgi-bin/text-idx?node=pt12.3.220

Federal Trade Commission

- Telemarketing Sales Rule
  https://www.ecfr.gov/cgi-bin/text-idx?node=pt16.1.310

USA PATRIOT Act

https://www.fincen.gov/resources/statutes-regulations/usa-patriot-act

- Section 314 – Cooperative Efforts to Deter Money Laundering
- Section 326 – Verification of Identification
- Section 352 – Anti-Money Laundering Programs

Overview of the Regulatory Framework

SRO Regulatory Requirements for Associated Persons

Registration and Continuing Education

SRO Qualification and Registration Requirements

All candidates for brokerage must have a **sponsoring broker** before they register to take a Series exam (though this is not the case for the Securities Industry Essentials exam). Usually, this occurs by means of a firm that has hired the candidate. The sponsoring firm needs to file an application form and pay processing fees with the **Central Registration Depository (CRD).** The applicant must submit their fingerprints through an approved facility (such as a local police station) and schedule their exam time.

Definition of Registered vs. Non-Registered Person

Registered persons are those who are registered with FINRA and participate in securities transactions. Examples of firm members who generally must be registered include salespeople, managers, partners, and directors. In order to be registered, the person must pass an exam and meet other requirements as established by FINRA.

A non-registered person is not registered with FINRA. However, depending on the circumstances, they may still be permitted to engage in limited activities. For example, individuals associated with a FINRA member are not required to be registered with FINRA if their role is only clerical or if they only facilitate transaction on a specific exchange with whom they are properly registered.

Permitted Activities of Registered and Non-Registered Persons

Persons registered with FINRA are permitted to engage in a variety of activities that vary depending on the person's qualifications. For example, a registered person who passes the Series 6 exam is permitted to engage in different activities compared with a registered person who passes the Series 7 exam.

According to "**NASD Notice to Members 00-50**," non-registered individuals are restricted in their ability to contact potential customers, being allowed to contact them for only three reasons:

- to invite the customer to events, sponsored by a registered firm, at which registered individuals will make solicitations
- to ask whether the customer would like to speak with a registered individual
- to determine whether the customer would like to receive literature from a registered firm

There are also restrictions on registered firms in their employment of non-registered individuals. They are not permitted to discuss investment products with customers or pre-qualify potential customers. Registered firms need to instruct such individuals on relevant regulations and penalties for noncompliance (including some amount of oversight to ensure compliance), and the firms need to perform background checks on them as well.

Moreover, non-registered persons, since they are not in the direct service of soliciting customers for investments, should be paid according to a salary or an hourly wage, not by commissions.

Ineligibility for Membership or Association

Ineligibility of certain persons for membership or association (Section 3) – no registered broker, dealer, municipal securities broker or dealer, or government securities broker or dealer can be a member if he fails to satisfy the qualification requirements. No person can be associated with a member if the person does not meet the qualification requirements. The Board has the authority to cancel a person's membership. If a member is found to be ineligible, the member can file an application for relief with the Board.

Background Checks

As registered persons have substantial responsibility, FINRA takes great care to closely check the backgrounds of applicants based on information submitted to the Central Registration Depository (CRD). FINRA considers whether the person is statutorily disqualified or whether they could represent an excessive risk to the industry. Member firms may also access the CRD to evaluate candidates.

Fingerprinting

Under **Rule 17(f)(2) of the Securities Exchange Act of 1934**, all partners, directors, officers, and employees of every member of a national securities exchange, broker, dealer, registered transfer agent, and registered clearing agency are required to be fingerprinted. The fingerprints are submitted to the United States Attorney General to be processed and maintained on file. There are some exceptions to this rule, however, such as employees who are not engaged in the sale of securities, employees who do not have regular access or do not regularly process securities or cash, and employees who do not have direct supervisory responsibility for employees with the responsibilities previously described.

The importance of this requirement lies in the ability that it provides for the United States government and regulatory organizations to identify members' employees and to help prevent fraudulent activity.

Statutory Disqualification

A statutory disqualification applies to a person:

1. when he/she is expelled or suspended from membership or participation in any self-regulatory organization,
2. when the Commission or other regulatory agency denies or suspends registration as or association with a broker-dealer for a period of time,
3. when the Commodity Futures Trading Commission denies, suspends, or revokes registration,
4. when a foreign financial regulatory authority denies, suspends, or revokes the person's authority to conduct transactions,
5. when conduct has been found to be a cause of any effective suspension or order by a domestic or foreign exchange or authority, or
6. when a person has associated himself or herself with another that is subject to a statutory disqualification and it was known or should have been known.

Filing of misleading information as to membership or registration (FINRA Rule 1122) – a member may not file information with FINRA having to do with membership or registration that is incomplete or inaccurate so as to be misleading. If a member does so, it is to be immediately corrected.

Failing to Register an Associated Person

Failure to register personnel (NASD IM-1000-3) – if a member fails to register an employee as a registered representative who should be so registered, it is found to be conduct inconsistent with just and equitable principles of trade and may be cause for disciplinary action.

Branch offices and offices of supervisory jurisdiction (NASD IM-1000-4) – a member is required to ensure that its membership application is kept current by means of supplementary amendments and to ensure that the main office is properly designated and registered, if required. A member is required to designate offices of supervisory jurisdiction and must register those branch offices.

State Registration Requirements

Investment advisers must register with the SEC, a self-regulatory agency (FINRA), and with the securities agency for the state where they principally conduct their business. Firms can register with FINRA, the SEC, and their state securities regulator using SEC Form BD (Uniform Application for Broker-Dealer Registration). Generally, the rule is that investment advisers who manage **over $100 million** in customer assets must register with the **SEC**, while those handling less must register with their **state securities agency**.

Investment advisers registering with the SEC are required to file the Form ADV Part 1A through **the Investment Adviser Registration Depository (IARD) system**, in addition to the submission of other documents.

There are some exemptions to the requirement for investment advisers to register with the SEC:

- if all the adviser's clients reside in the same state as the adviser's principal location of business,
- if the adviser provides no advice or reports concerning securities on a national securities exchange,
- if the adviser does not provide advisory service to a registered investment company or a business development security,
- if the adviser is servicing a charitable organization, or
- if the adviser is providing advice for church employee pension plans.

Retaking of Exams

A person whose registration has been terminated or revoked for a period of more than two years must retake the qualifying exam before they can be reinstated. A person must retake the SIE exam as well if a period of more than four years has elapsed.

Continuing Education (CE) Requirement

Firm Element

In terms of continuing education, there is a "brokerage firm element," which is a requirement for broker dealers to ensure that their employed RRs are up-to-date on various topics related to their particular jobs.

Regulatory Element

Among the continuing education requirements for RRs is to complete an exam covering various topics of regulation. This exam needs to be taken two years after one gains their license and then every three years after that.

Regarding the termination of a registered representative from his firm, a broker dealer is required to issue a form explaining the reason for the RR's departure, including the relevant ethical and legal factors.

Employee Conduct and Reportable Events

Employee Conduct

Form U4 and Form U5

The **Form U4** is the form filed by a prospective RR's sponsoring firm, outlining the applicant's **employment history** over the previous ten years. This must be exhaustive, explaining all of the applicant's full-time employment, part-time employment, unemployment, full-time education, and other things. Any gaps longer than three months are not permissible. The U4 also requires the applicant's residential history for the previous five years.

The **Form U5** is the form filed by a broker dealer upon a registered representative's **departure** from the firm. This form must explain any investigations, allegations, charges, litigation, regulatory actions, and customer complaints made against the RR. The U5 must be filed within thirty days, and the RR must be given a copy of it.

Purpose of Form U4

Form U4 (Uniform Application for Securities Industry Registration or Transfer) is used by broker-dealers to register associated persons with the proper self-regulatory organizations and jurisdictions. The form must be completed by all representatives of broker-dealers, investment advisers, and issuers of securities. Additionally, associated persons must complete a new Form U4 upon beginning work at a new broker-dealer, investment adviser, or issuer of securities. In addition to filing Form U4 upon commencing employment as an associated person, any material changes must also be disclosed by submitting an updated U4 in a timely manner.

Information That an Applicant Must Disclose on Form U4

Form U4 (Uniform Application for Securities Industry Registration or Transfer) requires the disclosure of a significant amount of personal, professional, and criminal information. Personal information that registrants must disclose includes general information such as name (including any name changes), height, weight, hair color, eye color, gender, birthplace, Social Security number, employment date with the current member firm, and five years of residential history. The professional information that must be disclosed includes any professional designations, 10 years of employment history, any outside business activities, and registration with unaffiliated firms. Finally, Form U4 also requires the disclosure of any criminal history or regulatory action or complaints brought against the person.

Purpose of Form U5

Form U5 (Uniform Termination Notice for Securities Industry Registration) is used by broker-dealers, investment advisers, or issuers of securities to terminate the registration of associated persons with the proper self-regulatory organizations and jurisdictions. Form U5 is only used in the case of a full termination. Upon a partial termination of only certain registrations or jurisdictions, the updates should be made using Form U4 (Uniform Application for Securities Industry Regulation or Transfer). If additional details relevant to Form U5 come to light after the initial filing of the form by the member firm, that member firm is obligated to electronically submit an amendment to Section 7 of Form U5.

Information That an Applicant Must Disclose on Form U5

Form U5 (Uniform Termination Notice for Securities Industry Registration) requires the disclosure of a significant amount of personal, registration, and termination information, as well as certain disclosures. Personal information that registrants must disclose includes general information such as name, Social Security data, general member firm identification information, and current residential address. The registration information that must be disclosed includes the nature of the termination (full or partial), the reason for termination, and the date of termination. Finally, the disclosure information requires the firm to disclose any investigations, internal reviews, criminal activities, or customer complaints and arbitration. Any affirmative disclosures within this section require the completion of an additional form (Internal Review Reporting Page) to provide further information.

Consequences of Filing Misleading Information or Omitting Information

In the event that a person files misleading or false information, or omits information of substance, their registration will be immediately invalidated regardless of their pass/fail status of their required exam. There may be other steps taken by the Financial Industry Regulator Authority (FINRA) and/or the Securities Exchange Commission (SEC), such as civil charges and fines.

FINRA, in order to help protect consumers from unscrupulous investment professionals, requires that individuals that are substantially involved in the administration of the securities industry be registered. Their registration implies an educational process that imparts the importance of following FINRA regulations. If an individual practices without registration, they (and any associated FINRA member) are liable to be subject to civil charges and fines, and to make restitution to customers for whom they transacted.

Customer Complaints

According to **FINRA Rule 4513, Records of Written Customer Complaints**, a **customer complaint** refers to any grievance by a customer or any person authorized to act on behalf of the customer involving the activities of the member or a person associated with the member in connection with the solicitation or execution of any transactions or the disposition of securities or funds of that customer. Each member is required to maintain for a period of at least four years copies of all such written customer complaints relating to that office and any actions taken by the member in response, including all related correspondence. Members who keep records in their office, instead of keeping records at the office of supervisory jurisdiction, must make such records promptly available at FINRA's request in such locations.

If a representative has communicated with a client and suspects that the client may have been stating a complaint, the representative must share that communication with their firm's chief compliance officer and/or compliance department. Compliance personnel will determine whether the customer communication should be treated as a complaint and will give guidance on the necessary steps to take in response. *Every* customer complaint should be investigated and addressed in a timely manner.

Official complaints must be in writing. Complaint forms can be filled out online on both the SEC website and the FINRA website. The SEC's Office of Investor Education and Advocacy (OIEA) receives many kinds of complaints from investors. Investors can submit a complaint form to OIEA to report problems with securities, representatives, or firms.

FINRA has different proceedings for handling customer complaints: formal and informal. The customer making the complaint decides whether to pursue formal or informal proceedings. If the customer decides to pursue **formal proceedings** to resolve their complaint, then the complaint must be resolved according to FINRA's **code of procedure**. According to this, the **District Business Conduct Committee (DBCC)** maintains first jurisdiction over complaints, and if the customer is dissatisfied with the DBCC's handling of the issue, they can appeal the outcome to the FINRA Board of Governors and even up to the Supreme Court.

If the customer decides to pursue **informal proceedings**, then the complaint can be resolved according to FINRA's **code of arbitration**. According to this, at least two arbiters will participate in an informal hearing, and their decision will be binding and not open to appeal. Arbitration can be pursued not only by customers, but by any members of FINRA, including complaints that RRs might have with broker-dealers.

Mediation is also available for complaints, where an independent third party provides a nonbinding resolution to the matter.

Potential Red Flags

A red flag is activity in a customer's account that may indicate misuse of the owner's money. This misuse may be on the part of the customer, such as money laundering, or on the part of the broker-dealer, like improper treatment of the customer's money by their registered representative.

FINRA requires that its members review accounts to monitor for red flags. This is most easily done with the use of exception reports. Exception reports compile lists of accounts that have recently experienced suspicious activity and make the information available to the FINRA member in one report so that they may focus on those accounts to determine if the red flags are an indication of actual misuse of customer funds.

How to Recognize a Red Flag or Complaint

Complaints are easily recognized. Complaints occur when customers inform the firm in writing if they take issue directly or tangentially with a securities transaction. Resolutions of complaints are obtained when the customer and FINRA firm agree on the resolution. In this case, the firm need only keep a record of the complaint, and no further escalation is required. If the firm and the customer cannot come to an agreement, the case will be escalated to FINRA for arbitration.

Red flags are usually identified via an exceptions report. It is vital that each red flag is investigated immediately to prevent fraud in a customer's account. The escalation process involves contacting the proper personnel until the issue is resolved. Such persons may include the account representative and/or registered principal among others.

Reportable Events

Outside Business Activities

Registered representatives are required to disclose **outside business activities** which would betray an "**adverse interest**" against the representative's own employer. RRs are permitted to execute trades for people employed at other firms, but they must exercise "**reasonable diligence**" to ensure that such trades do not unduly harm their own employers.

In case an RR does have an interest in an account at another firm, that firm is obligated to notify the RR's employer in writing, deliver duplicate documents for the account, and notify the RR of the completion of those tasks. This must be done before any transactions are conducted for the account.

Outside business activities can include personal investment accounts which the RR holds elsewhere than their own firm.

Private Securities Transactions

Private securities transactions are transactions where the broker sells a security not recognized or ordinarily sold by their own broker-dealer and/or receives compensation for the transaction. Such transactions are regulated, since registered representatives are forbidden from using their own brokerage firm as mere fronts for less safe transactions. If a broker engages in a private securities transaction which departs from established regulations (such as FINRA Rule 3040), then the broker commits the crime of "**selling away**."

Reporting of Political Contributions and Consequences for Exceeding Dollar Contribution Thresholds

The **Investment Advisers Act of 1940** prohibits investment advisers from providing their services to any government client for a period of two years following any political contribution they have made. And this rule applies not merely to those who make contributions to officials who are elected or to officials who later become elected, but to all officials who *may* become elected. Furthermore, advisers are forbidden from soliciting contributions for various officials or candidates if they are also pursuing or providing business with the government.

Dollar and Value Limits for Gifts and Gratuities and Non-Cash Compensation

The gifting of a very expensive item to a customer of a firm can be viewed as guaranteeing against loss or reimbursing losses. Both of these instances are illegal and unethical. Additionally, using expensive gifts as an inducement to buy securities is unethical and illegal. FINRA has explicit rules regarding gifting stated in FINRA Rule 3220. Associates may give up to $100 in value to each customer in a calendar year. Similarly, they may give or receive only $100 in value to other associates of other member firms. This is to prevent funneling business to other firms, which may not be in the customer's best interest. Exceptions to Rule 3220 include personal gifts, promotional items (i.e., pens, inexpensive desk decorations), and items that honor business deals (i.e., plaques) even if these articles surpass $100 in value.

Business Entertainment

Some FINRA members firms, such as open-end mutual funds companies, provide meals, tickets to entertainment venues, or reimbursement for travel and other expenses associate with attending conferences and seminars as inducement to sell their product. For the investment companies to provide these incentives, the following requirements should be met:

- The representative that accepts the compensation must have their firm's permission to attend the meeting,
- The firm must keep a record of any non-cash compensation that the representative receives,
- They do not receive reimbursement for recreational activities while at the meeting,
- The location of the meeting is in line with the purpose of the meeting,
- Reimbursement is not dependent upon a sales goal being reached, and
- There is no reimbursement for the representative's spouse to attend.

Felony, Financial-Related Misdemeanors, Liens, Bankruptcy

A member is required to report it within 30 calendar days if the member or an associated person:

- has violated any governing laws, rules, regulations, or standards of conduct
- is the subject of any written consumer complaint involving theft, misappropriation of funds or securities, or forgery
- is named as a defendant in a proceeding alleging violation of the Exchange Act of other governing legislation
- is denied registration or is expelled or otherwise disciplined by a regulatory body
- is indicted, convicted, or pleads guilty to any felony, or misdemeanor involving the purchase or sale of securities, taking of false oath, theft, larceny, robbery, and other pertinent misdemeanors

- is a director, controlling stockholder, or certain other officers of a broker, dealer, or investment company that was suspended, expelled, or had its registration denied or revoked
- is a defendant in certain securities, commodities, or financial related litigations
- is engaged in certain business transactions with a person that is statutorily disqualified as defined in the Exchange Act
- is subject to certain disciplinary action

A member is to report information regarding written customer complaints by the fifteenth day of the month after it was received.

Section 15 of the Securities Exchange Act of 1934 specifies a number of actions that could result in the limitation of activity or suspension, including:

- Willfully making a false or misleading statement or omission with respect to material facts within any application for registration or required reporting to the Commission
- A conviction within the preceding 10 years of any felony or misdemeanor involving the purchase or sale of securities, taking of a false oath, making of a false report, bribery, perjury, burglary, or conspiracy to commit such offenses
- A conviction within the preceding 10 years of any felony or misdemeanor involving the conduct of the business of a broker, dealer investment adviser, bank, insurance company, fiduciary, transfer agent, or ratings organization
- A conviction within the preceding 10 years of any felony or misdemeanor involving the larceny, theft, robbery, extortion, forgery, counterfeiting, fraudulent concealment, embezzlement, fraudulent conversion, or misappropriation of funds or securities
- Willfully violating or aiding and abetting the violation of the Securities Act of 1933, Investment Advisers Act of 1940, Investment Company Act of 1940, or Commodity Exchange Act.

Additional Rules and Regulations

In addition to the content included in this chapter, those sitting for the SIE Exam will need to be familiar with the following rules and regulations:

FINRA By-Laws

https://www.finra.org/rules-guidance/rulebooks/corporate-organization/laws-corporation

- Article I – Definitions
- Article III – Qualifications of Members and Associated Persons
- Article IV – Membership
- Article V – Registered Representatives and Associated Persons
- Article VI – Dues, Assessments, and Other Charges
- Article XII – Disciplinary Proceedings
- Article XV – Limitations of Power

FINRA Rules

- 0100 Series – General Standards
  https://www.finra.org/rules-guidance/rulebooks/finra-rules/0100
- 1000 Series – Member Application and Associated Person Registration
  https://www.finra.org/rules-guidance/rulebooks/finra-rules/1000
- 1122 – Filing of Misleading Information as to Membership or Registration
  https://www.finra.org/rules-guidance/rulebooks/finra-rules/1122
- 1240 – Continuing Education Requirements
  https://www.finra.org/rules-guidance/rulebooks/finra-rules/1240
- 2060 – Use of Information Obtained in Fiduciary Capacity
  https://www.finra.org/rules-guidance/rulebooks/finra-rules/2060
- 2263 – Arbitration Disclosure to Associated Persons Signing or Acknowledging Form U4
  https://www.finra.org/rules-guidance/rulebooks/finra-rules/2263
- 2267 – Investor Education and Protection
  https://www.finra.org/rules-guidance/rulebooks/finra-rules/2267
- 2310(c) – Non-cash Compensation
  https://www.finra.org/rules-guidance/rulebooks/finra-rules/2310
- 2320(g)(4) – Non-cash Compensation
  https://www.finra.org/rules-guidance/rulebooks/finra-rules/2320
- 2341(l)(5) – Non-cash Compensation
  https://www.finra.org/rules-guidance/rulebooks/finra-rules/2341
- 3110(e) – Responsibility of Member to Investigate Applicants for Registration
  https://www.finra.org/rules-guidance/rulebooks/finra-rules/3110
- 3220 – Influencing or Rewarding the Employees of Others
  https://www.finra.org/rules-guidance/rulebooks/finra-rules/3220
- 3270 – Outside Business Activities of Registered Persons
  https://www.finra.org/rules-guidance/rulebooks/finra-rules/3270
- 3280 – Private Securities Transactions of an Associated Person
  https://www.finra.org/rules-guidance/rulebooks/finra-rules/3280
- 4513 – Written Customer Complaints
  http://finra.org/rules-guidance/rulebooks/finra-rules/4513
- 4330 – Customer Protection – Permissible Use of Customers' Securities
  https://www.finra.org/rules-guidance/rulebooks/finra-rules/4330

- 4530 – Reporting Requirements
  https://www.finra.org/rules-guidance/rulebooks/finra-rules/4530
- 5110(h) – Non-cash Compensation
  https://www.finra.org/rules-guidance/rulebooks/finra-rules/5110
- 8312 – FINRA's BrokerCheck Disclosure
  https://www.finra.org/rules-guidance/rulebooks/finra-rules/8312

CBOE Rule

- 7.10 – Fingerprint-based Background Checks of Exchange Directors, Officers, Employees and Others
  https://markets.cboe.com/us/options/regulation/

MSRB Rules

- G-2 – Standards of Professional Qualifications
  http://www.msrb.org/Rules-and-Interpretations/MSRB-Rules/General/Rule-G-2.aspx
- G-3 – Professional Qualification Requirements
  http://www.msrb.org/Rules-and-Interpretations/MSRB-Rules/General/Rule-G-3.aspx
- G-7 – Information Concerning Associated Persons
  http://www.msrb.org/Rules-and-Interpretations/MSRB-Rules/General/Rule-G-7.aspx
- G-10 – Delivery of Investment Brochure
  http://www.msrb.org/Rules-and-Interpretations/MSRB-Rules/General/Rule-G-10.aspx
- G-20 – Gifts, Gratuities and Non-cash Compensations
  http://www.msrb.org/Rules-and-Interpretations/MSRB-Rules/General/Rule-G-20.aspx
- G-37 – Political Contributions and Prohibitions on Municipal Securities Business
  http://www.msrb.org/Rules-and-Interpretations/MSRB-Rules/General/Rule-G-37.aspx

SEC Rules and Regulations

- Securities Exchange Act of 1934
  http://legcounsel.house.gov/Comps/Securities%20Exchange%20Act%20Of%201934.pdf
    - Section 3(a)(39) – Definitions and Application of Title (Statutory Disqualification)
    - 17f-2 – Fingerprinting of Securities Industry Personnel

SIE Practice Test #1

Want to take this practice test in an online interactive format?
Check out the bonus page, which includes interactive practice questions and much more: **https://www.mometrix.com/bonus948/seriessie**

1. A registered principal or registered representative must retake the qualifying exam if his or her registration has been revoked or terminated for a period of _________ or more.

a. 1 year
b. 2 years
c. 3 years
d. 5 years

2. An options contract that gives the holder the right to purchase the number of shares of the underlying security is a _____________.

a. Put
b. Covered
c. Uncovered
d. Call

3. What are the three General Telemarketing Requirements as stated in FINRA Rule 3230?

a. Time of Day Restriction, State Do-Not-Call List, and National Do-Not-Call List
b. State Do-Not-Call List, National Do-Not-Call List, and Firm-Specific Do-Not-Call List
c. Time of Day Restriction, Firm-Specific Do-Not-Call List, and State Do-Not Call List
d. Time of Day Restriction, National Do-Not-Call List, and Firm-Specific Do Not Call List

4. Excessive trading in a customer's account for no apparent reason other than to generate commissions is ___________.

a. Churning
b. Rebalancing
c. Market-timing
d. Front-running

5. Which of the following is not a prohibited activity?

a. Rebalancing
b. Commingling funds
c. Guarantees against loss
d. Spreading market rumors

6. Any material for use in any newspaper, magazine, or other public medium, or by radio, television, or telephone recording, is referred to as ______________.

a. An advertisement
b. A market letter
c. A research report
d. Sales literature

7. What is the minimum time period that may be used in material promoting past records of research recommendations in connection with purchases or sales?

a. Six months
b. One year
c. Three years
d. Five years

8. Annual continuing education training provided by member firms is known as________.

a. Firm Continuing Education
b. Compliance Training
c. Firm Element Training
d. Firm Regulatory Training

9. Which of the following items does not need to be reported on Form U4?

a. Bankruptcy
b. DUI
c. Medical condition
d. Address change

10. Which of the following statements are true with respect to options communications that include historical performance?

a. A Registered Options Principal determines that the records or statistics fairly present the status of the recommendations or transactions reported upon
b. All relevant costs, including commissions, fees, and daily margin obligations, are disclosed and reflected in the performance
c. They must state that the results presented should not and cannot be viewed as an indicator of future performance
d. All of the above

11. Which of the following is false regarding collateralized mortgage obligation (CMO) advertisements?

a. Advertisements may not contain a comparison with any other investment vehicle.
b. Advertisements may contain comparisons with CDs.
c. Advertisements must include a description of the initial issue tranche.
d. Advertisements that contain an anticipated yield must disclose the prepayment assumption used to calculate the yield.

12. Which of the following items are required in a research report that contains ratings?

a. The meaning of each rating must be defined.
b. The percentage of all securities rated by the member to which the member would assign a "buy," "hold/neutral," or "sell" rating must be disclosed.
c. The member must disclose the percentage of subject companies within the "buy," "hold/neutral," and "sell" ratings for whom the member has provided investment banking services within the previous 12 months.
d. All of the above.

13. Which of the following written communications is considered a research report?

a. An email that includes an analysis of equity securities of individual companies
b. A discussion of broad-based indices
c. A commentary on economic, political, or market conditions
d. A technical analysis concerning the demand and supply for a sector, index, or industry based on trading volume and price

14. What is the limit of SIPC protection if a brokerage firm fails?

a. $100,000
b. $250,000
c. $500,000
d. $1,000,000

15. If a person has made lifetime gifts totaling $4,000,000 and dies in 2023, what is the amount that will be paid in taxes if the total remaining estate is $20,000,000?

a. $2,481,000
b. $4,377,800
c. $4,432,000
d. $4,968,000

16. What is the cost basis of securities received as an inheritance?

a. The current market price at the time the securities are received by the heir
b. The purchase price of the securities when they were originally bought
c. The market price on the date of death
d. The market price on the date of the original purchase

17. Which of the following securities are exempt from registration under the Securities Act of 1933?

a. Common stock
b. Municipal bond
c. Corporate bond
d. Preferred stock

18. ________ has the power to register, regulate, and oversee brokerage firms, transfer agents, and clearing agencies as well as SROs.

a. NASD
b. FINRA
c. SEC
d. MSRB

19. Which of the following item(s) can affect an investor's risk tolerance?

a. Age
b. Time frame
c. Personal experience
d. All of the above

20. Which of the following investments would not be considered appropriate for an investor with an objective of current income?

a. Growth stock
b. Municipal bond
c. Corporate bond
d. Utility stock

21. What is the tax advantage of owning municipal bonds?

a. No federal taxes
b. No state taxes regardless of your state of residence
c. No state taxes if the municipality is in your state of residence
d. Both A and C

22. __________ is the process of buying investment vehicles that have a high degree of uncertainty regarding their future value and expected earnings.

a. Speculation
b. Hedging
c. Gambling
d. Risk aversion

23. Which of the following scenarios would be considered an unsuitable recommendation?

a. Recommending a CD purchase to an elderly risk-averse investor
b. Recommending a common stock to a 30-year-old with a growth objective
c. Recommending a speculative stock to a recently retired investor who is risk averse
d. Recommending a growth stock mutual fund to a 30-year-old investor with a growth objective

24. If a registered representative receives a customer complaint, what should he or she do first?

a. Try to handle the customer by himself or herself
b. Notify the branch manager or designated compliance individual
c. Notify the Chief Compliance Officer of the broker-dealer
d. Nothing

25. Which of the following investments would be most suitable for a young investor who can only invest a small amount each month?

a. Common stock
b. Corporate bond
c. Options
d. Mutual fund

26. A corporate bond would be least suitable for which of the following investors?

a. A 25-year-old interested in speculative investments
b. A 25-year-old with an investment objective of growth and income
c. A retired individual with an investment objective of growth and income
d. A retired individual with an investment objective of income

27. In a community property state, how are assets divided between a husband and wife in a divorce?

a. 100% belongs to the husband
b. 100% belongs to the wife
c. 50% belong to the husband and 50% belong to the wife
d. 100% of the assets must remain jointly owned

28. Which of the following documents may be used to give a third party trading authorization on an account?

a. POA
b. TOD
c. Stock power
d. Account agreement

29. Which of the following information is not required as part of the requirement to know your customer?

a. Occupation and employer
b. Investment experience
c. Legal address
d. Level of education

30. In response to which event was the USA PATRIOT Act created?

a. The attack on Pearl Harbor on December 7, 1941
b. The bombing of the World Trade Center on February 26, 1993
c. The attack on the World Trade Center on September 11, 2001
d. The bombing of the Boston Marathon on April 15, 2013

31. All of the following are true regarding a suspicious activity report (SAR) except:

a. The deadline to file a SAR is 30 calendar days after becoming aware of any suspicious transaction or pattern of suspicious transactions or activities.
b. You are protected from civil liability when you report suspicious activity.
c. You are only required to file a SAR if you believe the activity is suspicious and involves $2,000 or more.
d. You must tell the person involved in the transaction that a SAR has been filed.

32. A type of mutual fund or exchange-traded fund (ETF) whose investment objective is to achieve approximately the same return as a specific market index, such as the S&P 500, is called a(n) _______________.

a. Value fund
b. Index fund
c. Balanced fund
d. Growth fund

33. Unsystematic risk is also known as ______________.

a. Market risk
b. Purchasing power risk
c. Credit risk
d. Diversifiable risk

34. The risk that a security will be redeemed prior to its maturity date is known as _______.

a. Market risk
b. Call risk
c. Event risk
d. Systematic risk

35. What type of bonds are high-risk securities that have received low ratings and produce high yields?

a. Junk bonds
b. Municipal bonds
c. Junior bonds
d. Convertible bonds

36. What is another name for an unrealized gain?

a. Paper profit
b. Capital gain
c. Capital loss
d. Hypothetical gain

37. If a company declares a 3:2 stock split, how many additional shares will an investor with 200 shares receive?

a. 100 shares
b. 200 shares
c. 400 shares
d. 600 shares

38. When interest rates increase, what happens to bond prices?

a. Bond prices increase
b. Bond prices decrease
c. Bond prices may increase or decrease
d. Changes in interest rate have no effect on bond prices

39. An option to buy shares of a new issue of common stock at a specified price, over a specified, fairly short period of time, is a __________.

a. Right
b. Warrant
c. Call
d. Put

40. Which of the following statements is false regarding short selling?

a. Money is made when prices fall.
b. Short selling carries high risk and a limited return.
c. Short selling carries low risk and an unlimited return.
d. Money is lost when prices rise.

41. What is the dividend amount that a shareholder who owns 100 shares will receive in the following scenario?

ABC Corporation declared a $0.25 dividend to shareholders of record on Monday, December 5, payable on December 15. The closing price of ABC Corporation stock on December 5 is $20.34.

a. $0.25
b. $2.50
c. $25.00
d. $250.00

42. Which of the following types of stocks are considered defensive stocks?

a. Public utilities
b. Gold mining
c. Technology companies
d. Both A and B

43. What is the tax rate on a long-term capital gain for an individual in the highest income tax bracket?

a. 10%
b. 15%
c. 20%
d. 25%

44. _______ represents the debts of a company.

a. Assets
b. Liabilities
c. Equity
d. Cash flow

45. Which financial statement provides a financial summary of the operating results of the company?

a. Income statement
b. Balance sheet
c. Cash flow statement
d. Annual report

46. ________ are municipal bonds backed by the revenue-generating capacity of the issuer.

a. Revenue bonds
b. General obligation bonds
c. Agency bonds
d. Treasury notes

47. Which of the following statements is true regarding a downward-sloping yield curve?

a. It indicates that yields tend to increase with longer maturities.
b. It indicates that rates for short- and long-term loans are essentially the same.
c. It indicates that intermediate term rates are the highest.
d. It indicates that short-term rates are higher than long-term rates.

48. If interest rates are expected to rise in the near future, which of the following statements is true regarding duration?

a. A longer duration would be preferred.
b. A shorter duration would be preferred.
c. There would be no preference regarding duration.
d. A mid-term duration would be preferred.

Use the following information to answer the next two questions.

Net profit after taxes:	$18,000	Stockholder's Equity:	$170,000
Total revenues:	$615,000	Preferred dividends:	$5,000
Total assets:	$340,000	Number of common shares outstanding:	3,800
Current assets:	$280,000	Current liabilities:	$85,000
Earnings per share:	$4.75	Market price:	$49.50

49. What is the net profit margin?

a. 10.59%
b. 10.42%
c. 2.92%
d. 3.29%

50. What is the P/E ratio?

a. 10.42
b. 10.59
c. 5.29
d. 3.29

51. What rating must a bond receive to be considered investment grade?

a. Aaa/AAA
b. Aa/AA
c. A/A
d. Baa/BBB

52. An order to buy a stock at specific price or better is what type of order?

a. Limit order
b. Stop order
c. Market order
d. Stop limit order

53. A stop limit order to sell 100 shares of ABC Corporation (ABC) stock at $35 is entered when the current market price of ABC stock is $45. The company announces lower-than-expected earnings and the stock price falls dramatically. Under which of the following scenarios will the order not execute?

a. The market price immediately falls to $35 and then rebounds to trade between $35 and $36 before falling below $35 again.
b. The market price immediately falls to $35 and continues to fall without rebounding.
c. The market price immediately falls to $35 and continues to trade between $33 and $36.
d. The market price immediately falls to $35 and continues to trade between $35 and $37.

54. How often must customers receive account statements from a brokerage firm?

a. Monthly, regardless of activity
b. Monthly, if activity, otherwise semiannually
c. Monthly, if activity, otherwise quarterly
d. Quarterly, regardless of activity

55. If an option expires without hitting its strike price, what happens to the buyer and seller?

a. The seller keeps the premium received and the buyer loses the premium paid.
b. The seller keeps the premium received and loses the shares of the underlying security.
c. The buyer loses the premium paid, but receives the shares of the underlying security.
d. Nothing happens.

56. What is the amount of the "catch-up" contribution to a traditional or Roth IRA that individuals aged 50 and over may make in 2023?

a. $500
b. $1,000
c. $1,500
d. $2,000

57. What is the tax consequence to an individual under the age of 59 ½ who withdraws a lump sum from his 401(k)?

a. The amount withdrawn is considered income and is subject to income taxes at the individual's rate.
b. The amount that is withdrawn is considered income and is subject to income taxes at the individual's current rate. Plus, he may be subject to a 10% penalty.
c. He must pay a 10% penalty. Otherwise, there are no tax consequences.
d. None of the above. A lump sum withdrawal from a 401(k) is not a taxable event.

58. Contributions made to a traditional or Roth IRA may consist of _________.

a. Cash only
b. Cash or securities
c. Cash, securities, or fine arts
d. Securities only

59. What are the tax consequences to an individual who converts a traditional IRA into a Roth IRA?

a. There are no tax consequences.
b. The amount converted is taxed as income at a flat rate of 15%.
c. The amount converted is taxed as income at a flat rate of 25%.
d. The amount converted is taxed as income at the individual's current tax rate.

60. What is the current yield of a 5% bond that is priced at 80?

a. 5.00%
b. 6.25%
c. 4.00%
d. 8.00%

61. What is the buying power in a margin account?

a. The amount of available cash
b. The amount of margin available to borrow
c. The amount of available cash plus the amount able to be borrowed
d. None of the above. Margin accounts do not have buying power.

62. If an investor writes a covered call and wishes to close the transaction, he needs to enter which of the following trades:

a. Sell to close
b. Buy to close
c. Sell to open
d. Both A and B

63. All of the following are true of an investor's rights in a rights offering except that

a. in the event the investor chooses to not purchase the shares offered, he or she may sell those rights to another investor.
b. the investor chooses to purchase the shares.
c. the investor's rights expire after 35 days due to the current market price dropping below the offering's subscription price.
d. all of the above are true.

64. Which of the following describe characteristics of a shareholder's preemptive rights?

a. In the event that the number of new shares proposed to be sold by the corporation causes the number of outstanding shares to outnumber the number of shares they are authorized to sell, the current shareholders must approve the increase to authorized shares before the sale can proceed.
b. Current shareholders are given the first option to purchase any new shares sold by a corporation.
c. Only after current shareholders have declined the offer to purchase shares from the corporation's new offering can the shares be offered for sale to the general investing public.
d. All of the above are true.

65. Which of the following terms can be described as the day the decision is made by the corporation's board of directors to provide the common stockholders with a dividend?

a. Declaration date
b. Record date
c. Ex-dividend date
d. None of the above

66. What are some characteristics of preferred stock?

a. Unless noted differently, par value for these shares is $1,000.
b. Ownership of these shares provides a means of fixed income for an investor through dividend payments.
c. Due to the fixed income nature of these shares, changes in interest rates have no effect on the price of these shares.
d. Maturity dates for these shares range from 1 to 25 years.

67. All of the following are true of the transferability of securities except that

a. securities can be transferred between parties by physically exchanging stock certificates.
b. a stock owner does not need the approval of the issuing organization of that stock to sell his or her shares.
c. the secondary market is where the transferring of securities is executed.
d. a broker dealer may assist in the transferring process of securities between two parties.

68. Of the different types of preferred stock, which one has the feature of enabling its owner to receive both the preferred and common dividend?

a. Cumulative preferred
b. Callable preferred
c. Participating preferred
d. Convertible preferred

69. Of the following, which is the LEAST likely to be utilized by economists in analyzing the overall condition of the economy?

a. Oil prices
b. Supply and demand
c. Gross domestic product (GDP)
d. Fluctuations in the country's business cycle

70. The stock market will be negatively impacted by all of the following except

a. an increase in taxation.
b. a money supply reduction.
c. an interest rate reduction.
d. reduced government spending.

71. When considering the four stages of an economic business cycle, which of the following are characteristics of the expansion stage?

I. Decline in savings
II. Real estate prices on the rise
III. An increase in gross domestic product (GDP)
IV. Rise in inventories

a. II, III, and IV
b. III only
c. II and III
d. I, II, and III

72. Which of the following is an example of a company in the defensive sector?

a. Manufacturing
b. Automobile
c. Computer
d. Pharmaceutical

73. What does a buy limit order do?

a. Allows an investor to set a maximum price he or she is willing to pay for a security
b. Allows an investor to set a minimum price at which he or she is willing to sell a security
c. Guarantees execution
d. All of the above

74. A specialist can handle all of the following types of orders except for

a. stop orders.
b. market orders.
c. AON orders.
d. buy limit orders.

75. What does security arbitrage involve?

a. Simultaneously buying and selling both a stock and a security that may be converted into that same underlying stock
b. Buying shares in a company that is being taken over or acquired while shorting shares in the company about to acquire them
c. Simultaneously buying and selling the same security in two different markets to exploit the price difference between the two
d. None of the above

Answer Key and Explanations for Test #1

1. B: A person whose registration has been terminated or revoked for a period of more than two years must retake the qualifying exam. A person must retake the SIE exam as well if a period of more than four years has elapsed.

2. D: A call is an option contract that gives the holder the right to purchase the number of shares of the underlying security. A put is an option contract that gives the holder the right to sell the number of shares of the underlying security. A covered option means that the option writer's obligation is secured by a specific deposit whereas an uncovered option means that the option writer's obligation is not secured.

3. D: The three General Telemarketing Requirements are the Time of Day Restriction, the Firm-Specific Do-Not-Call List and the National Do-Not-Call List.

4. A: Churning is excessive trading in a customer's account for no reason other than to generate commissions. Rebalancing refers to adjusting a customer's portfolio to return to previously set ratios of investment types. Market-timing is the practice of timing or calculating the market's low and high points, buying when it is low and selling when it is high. Front-running is an unethical, and generally illegal, activity in which a broker makes advantageous trades by using non-public information about an impending transaction.

5. A: Rebalancing is not a prohibited activity, while commingling funds, guaranteeing against loss, and spreading market rumors are prohibited.

6. A: The term advertisement refers to any material for use in any newspaper, magazine, or other public medium, or by radio, television, or telephone recording. A market letter, sometimes referred to as an investment newsletter, is a paid publication that focuses on a particular segment or type investments. A research report is typically a private report prepared for by an investment bank's research team for use by their customers. Sales literature is written material that outlines a product and its benefits, typically produced by the entity that is selling the product. Sales literature is often required to have a disclaimer noting the risks associated with investing.

7. B: Material promoting past records of research recommendations, in connection with purchases or sales, must cover at least a one-year time period.

8. C: The annual continuing education training provided by member firms is known as Firm Element Training. Firm Continuing Education and Firm Regulatory Training are not the correct terms for FINRA continuing education. Compliance Training is a general term for employee training mandated by legislation, regulation, or policy; it is not specific to Series license holders.

9. C: Medical conditions do not need to be reported on Form U4. A bankruptcy filing, DUI, and address change must be reported promptly on the registered representative's Form U4.

10. D: All of the statements are true with respect to options communications that include historical performance.

11. B: CMO advertisements may not contain comparisons with any other investment vehicle, including CDs.

12. D: A research report that contains ratings must define the meaning of each rating; the percentage of all securities rated by the member to which the member would assign a "buy," "hold/neutral," or "sell" rating must be disclosed; and the member must disclose the percentage of subject companies within the "buy," "hold/neutral," and "sell" ratings for whom the member has provided investment banking services within the previous 12 months.

13. A: An email that includes an analysis of equity securities of individual companies is considered a research report. Discussions of broad-based indices, commentaries on economic, political, or market conditions, and a technical analysis concerning the demand and supply for a sector, index, or industry based on trading volume and price are specifically excluded from the definition of a research report.

14. C: SIPC protects the securities and cash in a brokerage account up to $500,000 if a brokerage firm fails. The $500,000 protection includes up to $250,000 in cash in the brokerage account.

15. B: If a person has made lifetime gifts totaling $4,000,000 and dies in 2023, the amount that will be paid in taxes if the total remaining estate is $20,000,000 is $4,776,000. ($12,920,000 - $4,000,000 = $8,920,000 remaining exclusion amount; $20,000,000 - $8,920,000 = $11,080,000 taxable amount; $345,800 + $10,080,000 x 40% = $4,377,800.)

16. C: The cost basis of securities received as an inheritance is the market price on the date of death.

17. B: A municipal bond is exempt from registration, under the Securities Act of 1933, because it is issued by a government agency. Common stock, preferred stock, and corporate bonds are required to be registered because they are not issued by entities with high credit standing or by government agencies.

18. C: The SEC has the power to register, regulate, and oversee brokerage firms, transfer agents, and clearing agencies as well as SROs. The National Association of Securities Dealers (NASD), which existed from 1939 to 2007, oversaw the securities industry prior to the formation of FINRA. The Municipal Securities Rulemaking Board (MSRB) protects investors, issuers, and public pension plans by promoting a fair and efficient municipal market. The non-governmental agency known as FINRA (Financial Industry Regulatory Authority) governs registered agents and firms in the United States.

19. D: Age, time frame, and personal experience can all affect an investor's risk tolerance.

20. A: A growth stock would not be considered appropriate for an investor with an objective of current income. Older investors, or those who are looking for more conservative securities, prefer value stocks that pay dividends, CDs with predetermined interest and consistent payouts, or bonds that pay interest and cannot lose value. Younger investors would prefer growth, or aggressive, stocks because of the potential short-term gain if the stocks do well, since they have time to recover the invested amount if the stocks do poorly.

21. D: The tax advantage of owning municipal bonds is that they are not subject to federal taxes and also avoid state taxes if the municipality is in the investor's state of residence.

22. A: Speculation is the process of buying investment vehicles that have a high degree of uncertainty regarding their future value and expected earnings. Hedging is an investment strategy that seeks to reduce the impact of negative movements in price of a security. Gambling is fundamentally different from investing in that it relies entirely on chance. Risk-averse, or conservative, investors are those who are willing to settle for lower rates of return on their investments in exchange for a lower risk of losing the principal they have invested.

23. C: Recommending a speculative stock to a recently retired investor who is risk averse would be considered an unsuitable recommendation. Speculative, aggressive, or growth stocks would not be a good fit for older or retired investors that are risk averse. Older investors tend to be more conservative and are looking for stable income. Both common stocks and growth stock mutual funds are perfectly within a younger investor's goal for growth.

24. B: If a registered representative (RR) receives a customer complaint, the first thing he or she should do is notify the branch manager or designated compliance individual. FINRA Rule 4513 states that customer complaints must be submitted in writing and kept for at least four years on record. Complaints must be reported by the 15th day of the month.

25. D: A mutual fund would be the most suitable investment for a young investor who can only invest a small amount each month. Investing in the S&P 500 Index Fund would allow newer, younger investors to enjoy the outstanding performance of multiple companies without requiring outstanding investment knowledge or experience. Assuming that the young investor has little capital to invest in stocks and maintain a diversified portfolio, common stocks might leave the investor at a loss if other stocks perform better. Corporate bonds are better suited for conservative investors who are more concerned about steady income, as well as avoiding the risk of losing their initial investment. Options may be too complex for young investors who have no prior experience. Investing in options without proper knowledge could lead to overleveraging and speculation.

26. A: A corporate bond would be least suitable for a 25-year-old interested in speculative investments. Again, corporate bonds, and bonds in general, are better suited for conservative investors who are seeking steady, predetermined income.

27. C: In a community property state, when a husband and wife divorce, the assets are divided so that 50% belong to the husband and 50% belong to the wife.

28. A: A POA (power of attorney) document may be used to give trading authorization on an account to a third party.

29. D: A customer's level of education is not required as part of the requirement to know your customer (KYC).

30. C: The USA PATRIOT Act was enacted after the attack on the World Trade Center on September 11, 2001.

31. D: It is illegal to tell the person involved in the transaction that a SAR has been filed. The other three statements are true. The deadline to file a SAR is 30 calendar days after becoming aware of any suspicious transaction or pattern of suspicious transactions or activities. You are protected from civil liability when you report suspicious activity. You are only required to file a SAR if you believe the activity is suspicious and involves $2,000 or more.

32. B: A type of mutual fund or ETF whose investment objective is to achieve approximately the same return as a specific market index, such as the S&P 500, is called an index fund.

33. D: Unsystematic risk is also known as diversifiable risk. It results from random events such as labor strikes or lawsuits and affects various investment vehicles differently. It is this type of risk that can be eliminated through diversification.

34. B: The risk that a security will be redeemed prior to its maturity date is known as call risk. Market risk is the potential for loss due to the performance of the financial market. Event risk is the risk of an unexpected event negatively affecting an investment's value. Systematic risk is essentially the same as market risk.

35. A: Junk bonds (also called high yield bonds) are high-risk securities that have received low ratings and produce high yields. Municipal bonds are tax-exempt, so investors do not have to pay taxes on the interest from the bonds. A junior bond is corporate debt that, in the event of bankruptcy, will be repaid only after all other debts have been repaid. A convertible bond is a corporate bond that may be exchanged for stock in the company at maturity in lieu of receiving the face value as cash.

36. A: Paper profit is another name for an unrealized gain. If it was an unrealized loss, it would be called paper loss. A capital gain is a realized gain and a capital loss is a realized loss. Hypothetical gain is not a real term.

37. A: If a company declares a 3:2 stock split, an investor with 200 shares will receive an additional 100 shares of stock.

38. B: When interest rates increase, bond prices decrease. Bonds have an inverse relationship to interest rates. Most bonds pay a fixed interest rate that becomes more attractive if interest rates fall as there will be more investor demand that will drive up the price of the bond. Conversely, if interest rates rise, investors will no longer prefer the lower fixed interest rate paid by a bond, resulting in a decline in the price of the bond.

39. A: A right, as pertaining to a rights offering, is an option to buy one or more shares of common stock in a given company when new shares are issued, at a price initially below the market price, within a short timeframe, usually a month or less. A warrant is an option issued by a given company to buy one or more shares of common stock in that company at a price initially *above* the market price. Warrants are typically valid for multiple years. An option with the right to buy is known as a call option, and an option with the right to sell is known as a put option. Calls and puts are contracts made between participants in the marketplace rather than issued by a company.

40. C: Short selling does not carry low risk and an unlimited return. Short selling makes money when prices fall, it carries high risk, and it has a limited return. Short selling loses money when prices rise.

41. C: A shareholder who owns 100 shares will receive $25.00 (100 × 0.25). The price of the stock does not affect the dividend payout. Dividends are usually declared quarterly, though some companies may do it annually. A dividend yield would be the sum of the quarterly payouts (e.g. $0.25 × 4 = $1) divided by the current price of the stock (e.g. 1/25.34 = 0.039 = 3.9%).

42. D: Both public utility and gold mining stocks are considered defensive stocks. Technology companies are considered aggressive or growth investments.

43. C: The maximum tax rate on a long-term capital gain is 20% for an individual in the highest tax bracket. Long-term capital gains are the net sales on assets held for more than one year. For TY 2023, the highest tax bracket begins at income levels of $492,300 (Single), $553,850 (Married Filing Jointly), or $276,900 (Married Filing Separately).

44. B: Liabilities represent the debts of a company. Assets are resources held by the company that have immediate value or that will provide a future benefit. Equity represents the amount of stockholders' capital in a firm. Cash flow is the amount of cash moving into and out of a company.

45. A: The income statement provides a financial summary of the operating results of the company. The balance sheet is a summary report of a company's assets and liabilities, along with stockholder equity. The cash flow statement provides a summary of a company's cash flow and other events that caused changes in their cash position. An annual report is a document describing operations and financial position that every company listed on the stock market must provide to its shareholders.

46. A: Revenue bonds are municipal bonds backed by the revenue-generating capacity of the issuer. Municipal bonds backed by the full faith and credit, and taxing power, of the issuer are called general obligation bonds. Agency bonds are issued by either an agency of the US government (other than the Treasury) or a government-sponsored enterprise (GSE) and may not be fully guaranteed. Treasury notes are bonds issued by the US Treasury and are backed by the full faith and credit of the US government.

47. D: An inverted, or downward-sloping, yield curve indicates that short-term rates are higher than long-term rates. A normal, upward-sloping yield curve indicates that yields tend to increase with longer maturities. A flat yield curve indicates that interest rates are similar across all available terms. A humped, or bell-shaped, curve indicates that medium-term (intermediate) rates are higher than either short- or long-term rates.

48. B: If interest rates are expected to rise in the near future, a shorter duration would be preferred. A longer duration would be preferred if interest rates are expected to fall.

49. C: The net profit margin is 2.92% (18,000/615,000).

50. A: The P/E ratio is 10.42 (49.50/4.75).

51. D: To be considered investment grade, a bond must receive a rating of at least Baa/BBB. Aaa/AAA and Aa/AA are the highest credit ratings, meaning these bonds are high quality investment grade. A/A is better than Baa/BBB, so these bonds are still investment grade.

52. A: An order to buy or sell a stock at a specific price or better is a limit order. A market order is an order to buy or sell at the best available price at the time the order is placed. A stop is an order to buy or sell a stock when its market price reaches or drops below a specified price. A stop limit order is an order to buy or sell at a specific price or better once a given stop price has been hit.

53. B: When the market price of ABC stock hits $35, the stop has been met and the order turns into a limit order to sell at $35 or higher. Since the market price continued to fall and stayed below $35, the limit order did not execute. In answers A, C, and D, the market price rose above the limit order price of $35. Therefore, those orders would execute.

54. C: Customers must receive account statements from brokerage firms at least every quarter. Often, firms will send monthly statements to account holders with any activity.

55. A: If an option expires without hitting its strike price, the seller keeps the premium received and the buyer loses the premium paid.

56. B: In TY 2023, the catch-up contribution to a traditional or Roth IRA that individuals aged 50 and over may make is $1,000, bringing the maximum total contribution amount for these individuals up to $7,500.

57. B: The tax consequence to an individual under the age of 59 ½ who withdraws a lump sum from a 401(k) is that the amount that is withdrawn is considered income and is subject to income taxes at the individual's current rate. The individual may also be subject to a 10% penalty for early withdrawal.

58. A: Contributions made to a traditional or Roth IRA may consist of cash only. Securities or fine arts may not be contributed to a traditional or Roth IRA. Any non-cash assets in a non-retirement brokerage account that are to be transferred to a retirement account, must first be liquidated (sold) so they can be transferred in as cash.

59. D: The tax consequences to an individual who converts a traditional IRA into a Roth IRA are that the amount converted is counted as income and is subject to the individual's current tax rate.

60. B: Bonds by default have a par value (also face value or nominal value) of $1,000, but bonds might trade for more or less, in which case they would be priced or quoted at some percentage of that. In this case, a bond that is priced at 80 would sell for $800. The percent tied to a bond is its coupon, and it is stated in terms of the par value. In this case, a bond with a 5% coupon, which can be called a 5% bond, would issue regular coupon payments of 5% of its par value, or $50.

Since the current yield of a bond refers to the actual interest income produced by that bond relative to the bond's market (not par) price, the current yield of a 5% bond priced at 80 would be $50 / $800 = 6.25%.

61. C: The buying power in a margin account is the amount of available cash plus the amount able to be borrowed. This is also called purchasing power.

62. D: If an investor has a covered call, this means that he has sold a call option to a third party and simultaneously has ownership of the underlying security for that option, e.g. selling a call option to purchase ABC stock while simultaneously owning (or buying) ABC stock. Accordingly, to close out this position, the investor would have to reverse both sides of this position, buying back the call option and selling the underlying security; this is then a combination of buying to close and selling to close.

63. C: Investors' rights expire only after 45 days. Additionally, investors may choose to exercise the rights to purchase additional shares or sell those rights to another investor who would like to buy those shares.

64. D: A shareholder's preemptive rights provide for him or her to receive the first option to purchase shares from any new offering conducted by the corporation, provide for the shares to be offered to the public only after they've been declined by the current shareholders, and require approval from the current shareholders for any increase to the number of the corporation's authorized shares.

65. A: The declaration date is the date when the board of directors declares the decision to pay out a dividend to common stockholders of record. The record date is when investors must be officially recorded as stockholders on stock certificates in order to qualify for receipt of the declared dividend. The ex-dividend date is the first day that the stock trades without the declared dividend attached and, accordingly, will not be given to anyone purchasing the stock as of this date or after.

66. B: Ownership in preferred stock provides a fixed income to the investor through dividend payments. The par value of shares is generally $100, not $1,000. Due to the fixed income nature of these shares, they are more sensitive to changes in interest rates, demonstrating an inverse relationship between rates and pricing. These shares have no maturity date and are therefore considered perpetual.

67. A: Securities are transferable only after the owner either endorses the stock certificates or signs a power of substitution into the new owner's name. Owners may sell shares without the approval of the requisite issuing organization, securities transfers are executed in the secondary market, and broker dealers assist in the securities transferring process.

68. C: Participating preferred stock ownership provides the investor the right to receive both the preferred and common dividend when paid. Cumulative preferred shares not only allow the owner payment of the preferred dividend but also provide protection against missed dividend payments by requiring back payment of those dividends. Callable shares afford the corporation the right to call in those shares, often at a premium price. Convertible shares allow for the option to exchange preferred shares for common shares at a conversion price.

69. A: In analyzing the overall condition of a country's economy, an economist would be least likely to utilize oil prices, and MORE likely to look to charts and models regarding supply and demand, the country's gross domestic product (GDP), and fluctuations in its business cycle.

70. C: Falling interest rates will have a positive effect on stock market performance. An increase in taxes, or a reduction in the money supply or government spending, will negatively impact the stock market.

71. C: With regards to the stages of an economic business cycle, the expansion stage would be characterized by a rise in real estate prices and an increase in gross domestic product (GDP). A decline in the amount and rate of savings and a rise in inventories would be characteristics of the contraction stage.

72. D: A pharmaceutical company would be categorized as defensive, providing products that are needed and will be purchased by individuals regardless of the state of the economy. Manufacturing and automobile companies would be cyclical, and a computer company would be growth.

73. A: A buy limit order allows protection to an investor by providing the chance to set a maximum price they are willing to pay for a security. A sell limit order allows an investor to set a minimum price at which he or she is willing to sell a security. A buy limit order provides price protection to the investor in that it guarantees he or she will not pay over a certain price for that security, but accordingly, it will NOT guarantee execution of that order in the event that the price level of that security does not reach the investor's desired price or below.

74. B: A specialist cannot accept market orders in that the nature of those types of orders dictates that they be executed as soon as they are presented to the market, and accordingly, there would be at that point no order to leave with the specialist.

75. A: Security arbitrage involves the simultaneous purchase and sale of both a stock and a security that may be converted into that same underlying stock. Buying shares in a company that is being taken over or acquired, while shorting shares in the company about to acquire them, is risk arbitrage. Simultaneously buying and selling the same security in two different markets in order to exploit the price difference between the two is market arbitrage.

SIE Practice Test #2

1. Within how many days must a member report to FINRA if the member or an associated person of the member is the subject of a written customer complaint involving allegations of theft or misappropriation of funds?

a. 10 business days
b. 15 calendar days
c. 20 business days
d. 30 calendar days

2. Correspondence means any written communication that is distributed to ____ or fewer retail investors within any _____-day period.

a. 10 or fewer investors within any 10-day period
b. 15 or fewer investors within any 20-day period
c. 25 or fewer investors within any 30-day period
d. 30 or fewer investors within any 25-day period

3. What is the dollar value that any gift from or to a member or person associated with a member may not exceed in one year?

a. $0 (gifts are not allowed)
b. $50
c. $100
d. $200

4. A registered representative trading an equity based on non-public information in his or her own account before trading for clients is called _____________.

a. Churning
b. Rebalancing
c. Market timing
d. Front running

5. Which of the following items regarding SIPC must member firms advise all new customers of in writing when opening a new account?

I. The SIPC website address
II. The SIPC telephone number
III. How to obtain the SIPC brochure

a. I only
b. I and III
c. I and II
d. I, II, and III

6. Which of the following terms refers to printed or processed analysis covering individual companies or industries?

a. Advertisement
b. Market letter
c. Research report
d. Sales literature

7. When using testimonials, which of the following points does not need to be clearly stated in the body copy of the material?

a. The testimonial may not be representative of the experience of other clients.
b. The fact that that it is a paid testimonial if a nominal sum is paid.
c. If the testimonial concerns a technical aspect of investing, the person making the testimonial must have adequate knowledge and experience to form a valid opinion.
d. The testimonial cannot be indicative of future performance or success.

8. Registered Investment Advisers are registered through the ________.

a. FINRA
b. SEC
c. MSRB
d. NYSE

9. Prior to the Options Disclosure Document (ODD) being delivered, a registered representative may do which of the following:

a. Solicit a sale of an options contract as long as the ODD is sent before or at the time of sale
b. Place an options trade for a client's account as long as the ODD is sent the same day
c. Place an options trade for a client's account as long as the ODD is sent before settlement
d. Limit discussions to general descriptions of the options

10. A municipal security advertisement that concerns the facilities, services, or skills with respect to municipal securities of such broker, dealer, or municipal securities dealer or of another broker, dealer, or municipal securities dealer is the definition of __________.

a. Professional advertisement
b. Product advertisement
c. New issue product advertisement
d. Municipal fund security product advertisement

11. A member may not publish a research report regarding a subject company for which the member acted as manager or co-manager of an IPO for _______ days following the date of the offering.

a. 20 calendar days
b. 20 business days
c. 40 calendar days
d. 40 business days

12. Which of the following is true regarding third-party research reports?

a. A third-party research report is a research report produced by a person in the research department of a member firm.
b. Third-party research reports and independent third-party research reports have the same meaning.
c. A registered principal (or supervisory analyst) must approve all third-party research reports distributed by a member.
d. A registered principal (or supervisory analyst) must approval all independent third-party research reports.

13. Which of the following accounts is not covered by FDIC?

a. Bank savings and checking accounts
b. Mutual fund account
c. Bank money market account
d. Certificates of deposit

14. What is the limit of FDIC protection per depositor, per insured bank, for each account ownership category?

a. $100,000
b. $250,000
c. $500,000
d. $1,000,000

15. What is the maximum amount that may be gifted within one calendar year (2023) to avoid taxation?

a. $14,000
b. $15,000
c. $16,000
d. $17,000

16. A ____________ refers to when a company first sells it shares to the public.

a. Initial public offering
b. Initial marketing
c. Initial sales offering
d. Initial rights offering

17. The SEC was created under __________.

a. The Securities Act of 1933
b. The Securities Exchange Act of 1934
c. Investment Company Act of 1940
d. Investment Advisers Act of 1940

18. Which of the following financial information is not required on a new account application?

a. Net worth
b. Annual income
c. Liabilities
d. Liquid net worth

19. The length of time an investor plans to keep an investment is known as the ________.

a. Holding period
b. Time horizon
c. Quiet period
d. Calendar period

20. Which of the following investments would not be appropriate for an investor with a capital growth objective?

a. Unit investment trust
b. Common stock
c. Growth mutual fund
d. Zero coupon bond

21. Investing in multiple investment vehicles within a portfolio to reduce risk or increase returns is called ___________.

a. Dollar cost averaging
b. Discounting
c. Diversification
d. Distribution

22. _________ risk refers to the impact that bad management decisions, other internal missteps, or external situations can have on a company's performance and on the value of investments in that company.

a. Market
b. Investment
c. Financial
d. Management

23. Under Regulation T, what is the maximum amount of the total purchase price of a stock for new purchases that a firm can lend a customer?

a. 25%
b. 50%
c. 75%
d. 100%

24. How often must firms notify employees of their business continuity or disaster recovery plans?

a. Annually
b. Semiannually
c. Quarterly
d. Monthly

25. Which of the following investments would be most suitable for an investor in a high tax bracket who wants to avoid paying any taxes on his investments?

a. Corporate bond
b. Municipal bond
c. Mutual fund
d. Preferred stock

26. What is margin in a brokerage account?

a. The difference between the purchase price and the current value of each security.
b. The difference between the beginning value and the current value of the entire account.
c. Borrowed money that is used to purchase securities.
d. Purchasing power in a cash account.

27. At what age does a UTMA account terminate?

a. 18
b. 19
c. 20
d. 21

28. __________ trading authority is when a person other than the account holder may invest without consulting the account holder about the price, amount, or type of security or the timing of the trades that are placed for the account.

a. Discretionary
b. Nondiscretionary
c. Privileged
d. Absolute

29. Which of the following would be a red flag when opening an account for a new client?

a. No investment experience
b. High annual income, but little or no savings
c. Hesitant to give financial information
d. Nervous or anxious when answering questions about objectives for the account

30. Dividing a larger transaction into smaller transactions to avoid triggering a reporting or recordkeeping requirement is called ________.

a. Layering
b. Fraud
c. Structuring
d. Laundering

31. Which of the following persons are considered corporate insiders?

a. Officers
b. Directors
c. Employees
d. All of the above

32. Systematic risk is also known as ____________.

a. Market risk
b. Credit risk
c. Liquidity risk
d. Interest rate risk

33. What type of risk involves the chance that Congress will make unfavorable changes in tax laws?

a. Market risk
b. Event risk
c. Tax risk
d. Liquidity risk

34. Which of the following terms is a maneuver used by a company that increases the number of shares outstanding by exchanging a specified number of new shares of stock for each outstanding share?

a. Stock dividend
b. Stock split
c. Stock valuation
d. Stock buyback

35. Investing a fixed dollar amount in a security at fixed intervals is known as _________.

a. Asset allocation
b. Diversification
c. Budgeting
d. Dollar cost averaging

36. What is the name of the strategy where a company reduces the number of shares outstanding by exchanging a fractional amount of a new share for each outstanding share of stock?

a. Stock dividend
b. Stock split
c. Reverse stock split
d. Reverse stock dividend

37. If a company declares a 1:2 reverse stock split, how many shares will an investor with 200 shares own after the split?

a. 100 shares
b. 200 shares
c. 300 shares
d. 400 shares

38. _________ is an intangible asset that is the result of the acquisition of one company by another for a premium value.

a. Target value
b. Book value
c. Acquisition value
d. Goodwill

39. Which of the following characteristics are true of preferred stocks?

I. Have a prior claim on the income and assets of the issuing firm
II. Have fixed dividends
III. Issued as an alternative to debt
IV. Have an effect on EPS

a. I and II
b. I and III
c. I, II, III
d. I, II, III, IV

40. Dollar-denominated negotiable receipts for company stock of a foreign company held in trust in a foreign branch of a U.S. bank are ____________.

a. IPOs
b. ADRs
c. AMTs
d. ATMs

41. Assuming rational market behavior, what should the opening price of ABC Corporation be on December 6?

On Monday, December 5, after trading for that day ceased, ABC Corporation declared that it would pay an unanticipated $0.25 dividend, payable on December 15. The December 5 closing price of ABC Corporation stock is $25.34

a. $25.34
b. $25.09
c. $25.59
d. Not enough information given

42. An investor who owns 200 shares of XYZ Company, which is currently trading at $25.00, will be receiving a 20% stock dividend. What will the investor receive on the payment date?

a. $1,000
b. $100
c. 20 shares of XYZ stock
d. 40 shares of XYZ stock

43. How long must you hold an investment for it to be considered long term?

a. 6 months
b. 1 year
c. 1 year and 1 day
d. 2 years

44. What represents the amount of stockholders' capital in a firm?

a. Assets
b. Liabilities
c. Equity
d. Cash flow

45. Which financial statement provides a summary of the firm's cash flow and other events that caused changes in the cash position?

a. Income statement
b. Balance sheet
c. Cash flow statement
d. Annual report

46. What is the graph called that represents the relationship between a bond's term to maturity and its yield at a given point in time?

a. Efficient frontier
b. Point and figure chart
c. Yield curve
d. Bar chart

47. Which of the following mutual funds would be most likely to be passively managed?

a. Bond fund
b. Growth fund
c. Income fund
d. Index fund

48. An account in which customers with large portfolios pay a brokerage firm a flat annual fee that covers the cost of a money manager's services and the cost of commissions is called a ________ account.

a. Cash
b. Margin
c. Collateral
d. Wrap

Use the following information to answer the next two questions.

Net profit after taxes:	$18,000	Stockholder's Equity:	$170,000
Total revenues:	$615,000	Preferred dividends:	$5,000
Total assets:	$340,000	Number of common shares outstanding:	3,800
Current assets:	$280,000	Current liabilities:	$85,000
Earnings per share:	$4.75	Market price:	$49.50

49. What is the current ratio?

a. 2.92%
b. 3.29%
c. 5.29%
d. 10.59%

50. What is the book value per share?

a. $29.58
b. $43.42
c. $44.74
d. $46.10

51. Which of the following is the over-the-counter market?

a. NYSE
b. NASDAQ
c. CBOE
d. CBT

52. Which of the following is an example of a limit order?

a. An order to sell 100 shares of XYZ at the best price available
b. An order to sell 100 shares of XYZ (currently trading at $50) if the price drops to $45
c. An order to buy 100 shares of XYZ at the best price available
d. An order to buy 100 shares of XYZ at $40 or less

53. Which of the following is not required on an order ticket?

a. Customer name
b. Account number
c. Order type
d. Symbol

54. A stock trade executed on Friday, January 2, will settle on what date?

a. Monday, January 5
b. Tuesday, January 6
c. Wednesday, January 7
d. Thursday, January 8

55. In 2023, what is the maximum contribution that a 45-year-old may make into a traditional IRA?

a. $2,000
b. $3,500
c. $6,500
d. $7,500

56. What is the maximum annual contribution amount allowed in a Coverdell Education Savings Account (CESA)?

a. $500
b. $2,000
c. $5,500
d. $14,000

57. What is the tax consequence to an individual over the age of 59 ½ who withdraws a lump sum from his 401(K)?

a. The amount withdrawn is considered income and is subject to income taxes at the individual's rate.
b. The amount that is withdrawn is considered income and is subject to income taxes at the individual's current rate. Plus, he may be subject to a 10% penalty.
c. He must pay a 10% penalty. Otherwise, there are no tax consequences.
d. None of the above. A lump sum withdrawal from a 401(K) is not a taxable event.

58. How are capital gains and losses inside an IRA reported on an individual's income taxes each year?

a. Neither gains nor losses within an IRA reported.
b. Gains are not reported, but losses are reported on a Form 1099B to be used as a deduction.
c. Both gains and losses are reported on Form 1099B.
d. Gains and losses in an IRA are both reported on Form 1099B, but they are not subject to taxation.

59. An individual converts his $100,000 traditional IRA into a Roth IRA just before a major market decline causes the value to drop to $50,000. This investor should ____________ the Roth IRA back to a traditional IRA to avoid paying taxes on the extra $50,000.

a. De-convert
b. Roll over
c. Recharacterize
d. Transfer

60. An option that is written against stock owned is a/an ________ option.

a. Naked
b. Covered
c. Open
d. Closed

61. How are gains and losses on options treated for tax purposes?

a. They are treated as long-term gains or losses.
b. They are treated as short-term gains or losses.
c. They may be treated as either short-term or long-term gains or losses.
d. Gains and losses on options are not taxable.

62. Which of the following statements are true regarding real estate investment trusts (REITs)?

a. They are professionally managed.
b. Allows smaller investors to participate in capital appreciation and income returns of real estate without owning any property.
c. Returns can be very volatile.
d. All of the above.

63. Which of the following corporate issues does an investor have the right to vote on as a common stockholder?

a. Proposed stock splits
b. Corporate bond issuance
c. Election of the board of directors
d. All of the above

64. All of the following are true of stockholder voting methods except that

a. the statutory method involves an investor voting equal amounts of his or her votes for each of the candidates they would like to vote for.
b. special circumstances may allow for a stockholder to vote more than one vote per share for each share he or she owns.
c. the cumulative method involves an investor choosing to cast all of his or her votes for one candidate.
d. there are two methods by which stockholders may cast their votes.

65. Which of the following describe the rights shareholders possesses?

I. They retain an interest in residual assets that is proportionate to their investment in the event the corporation declares bankruptcy.
II. They can access a corporation's financial information that would be otherwise held as confidential.
III. They receive a shareholder list.
IV. They can inspect a corporation's books and records.

a. II, III, and IV
b. I, III, and IV
c. I, II, and IV
d. III and IV

66. Which of the following is NOT true regarding the options of an investor who possesses a warrant to purchase common stock?

a. The investor must exercise the warrant before the stock's price rises above the subscription price.
b. The investor may sell the warrant to another investor.
c. The investor may exercise the warrant at any time prior to expiration to purchase common stock at the warrant's subscription price.
d. all of the above statements are true.

67. Which of the following duties does a transfer agent NOT perform?

a. Maintains the list of stockholders
b. Verifies owner identity in stock issuance
c. Verifies the validity and legality of a company's debt in a bond issuance
d. Handles new issuance of stock certificates

68. Which of the following economic indicators would be classified as a leading indicator?

I. Stock market prices
II. Corporate profit and loss
III. Permits to build
IV. Changes in borrowing (businesses and consumers)

a. I, II, III, and IV
b. I only
c. I, III, and IV
d. I and II

69. When considering a corporation's balance sheet, all of the following are categorized as *other assets* EXCEPT

a. trademarks.
b. patents.
c. property.
d. goodwill.

70. Of the following terms, which represents simply the value of a country's produced goods and services?

a. Disintermediation
b. Gross domestic product (GDP)
c. Real gross domestic product (RGDP)
d. Consumer price index (CPI)

71. Which of the following would be associated with the government's efforts to slow down the economy?

I. Reduction in taxes
II. Reduction spending
III. Increase in taxes
IV. Increase in spending

a. I and II
b. II and III
c. III and IV
d. I and IV

72. What is an order that enables the broker to have discretion regarding the timing of its execution and price called?

a. Fill-or-kill order
b. All-or-none order
c. Market-on-open order
d. Not-held order

73. An investor has sold short 275 shares of stock PPG at $26 per share. The market currently has PPG trading at $11 per share. The investor sees news of the company that may indicate a price increase over the short term. Which of the following would provide this investor with guaranteed protection against missing a purchase of PPG at a level at which he or she can still make a profit given the short position?

a. Buy 275 PPG at $21 stop
b. Unknown without more information
c. Buy 275 PPG at $32 stop
d. None of the above

74. When orders have the same price, what is the order of prioritization for executing each?

I. Parity
II. Precedence
III. Priority

a. I and II
b. II, I, and III
c. III, II, and I
d. I, II, and III

75. Which of the following are considered to be actions falling under the role of a dealer?

I. Charges a commission for their services
II. Participates in the trade by trading in and out of his or her own account
III. Fills the role of market maker
IV. May facilitate only the order execution for a customer

a. II only
b. I, II, and III
c. I and IV
d. II and III

Answer Key and Explanations for Test #2

1. D: A member shall promptly report the complaint, no later than 30 calendar days after the member knows or should have known of the existence of the written complaint.

2. C: Correspondence means any written communication (including electronic) that is distributed to 25 or fewer retail investors within any 30-day period.

3. C: Any gift from or to a member or person associated with a member may not exceed $100 per year.

4. D: Front running is the prohibited activity of a registered representative trading based on non-public information in his or her own account prior to the information becoming public to other traders. Market timing is the practice of timing or calculating the market's low and high points, buying when it is low and selling when it is high. Rebalancing refers to adjusting a customer's portfolio to return to previously set ratios of investment types. Churning involves a broker, or someone trading on behalf of a customer, processing excessive transactions with the goal of increasing their commissions from trades.

5. D: Member firms must disclose, in writing, to all new customers that they may obtain more information about SIPC, including the brochure, by contacting SIPC and must also provide the website address and telephone number of SIPC.

6. C: The term research report refers to printed or processed analysis covering individual companies or industries.

7. B: If only a nominal sum is paid, the body copy of the material does not need to clearly state that it is a paid testimonial. If more than a nominal sum is paid, however, the fact that it is a paid testimonial must be indicated.

8. B: Investment firms and advisers are required to register with the SEC, FINRA, and the office of the securities regulator of the state in which they are doing business. Firms and advisors can register for all three using SEC Form BD.

9. D: Prior to the Options Disclosure Document (ODD) being delivered, a registered representative must limit discussion to general descriptions of the options. Solicitations and trades are not allowed prior to delivery of the ODD.

10. A: A municipal security advertisement that concerns the facilities, services, or skills with respect to municipal securities of such broker, dealer, or municipal securities dealer or of another broker, dealer, or municipal securities dealer is the definition of a professional advertisement.

11. C: A member may not publish a research report regarding a subject company for which the member acted as manager or co-manager of an IPO for40 calendar days following the date of the offering.

12. C: A registered principal (or supervisory analyst) must approve all third-party research reports distributed by a member. A registered principal (or supervisory analyst) does not need to approve independent third-party research reports.

13. B: A mutual fund account is covered by SIPC rather than FDIC. Bank savings, checking, and money market accounts as well as certificates of deposits are covered by FDIC.

14. B: The FDIC covers up to $250,000 per depositor per insured bank for each account ownership category. The SIPC protects customers of brokerage firms up to a total of $500,000 across all accounts but not per account.

15. D: In TY 2023, $17,000 is the maximum amount that may be gifted within one calendar year to avoid taxation.

16. A: An initial public offering refers to the event of a company first offering its shares for sale to the public. Market offerings and initial sales offerings are not generally accepted terms for this event. A rights offering refers to a group of rights, a kind of option, offered to shareholders to purchase more shares.

17. B: Congress created the Securities and Exchange Commission (SEC) under the Securities Exchange Act of 1934. The Securities Act of 1933 regulates the stock market. The Investment Company Act of 1940 regulates the organization of investment companies. The Investment Advisers Act of 1940 defines an investment advisor.

18. C: Liabilities are not required financial information on a new account application. Net worth, annual income, and investment goals are required pieces of financial information to open a brokerage account with any firm.

19. B: The length of time an investor *plans* or *expects* to keep an investment is known as the time horizon. The holding period refers to the length of time that an asset is *actually* held. During an IPO process, the SEC restricts the marketing department of the company from publicizing any information about the IPO to avoid insider trading. Calendar period does not refer to any specific investment concept.

20. D: A zero coupon bond would not be appropriate for an investor with a capital growth objective. Bonds and annuities are better suited for investors with a conservative or fixed income objective. Unit investment trusts are similar to mutual funds in that they offer a variety of portfolios to invest in, including growth. Common stocks are perfect for growth investors as they provide the opportunity to invest directly in the company to maximize capital gains. Growth mutual funds offer investors a single price for a growth-focused portfolio consisting of any number of companies.

21. C: Investing in multiple investment vehicles within a portfolio to reduce risk or increase returns is called diversification. An investor engages in dollar-cost averaging by purchasing a fixed-dollar amount of a given security at set intervals, such as monthly, to smooth out the volatility. Discounting involves calculating the net present value of a distribution of funds that is to take place in the future. A distribution is the payout (interest, dividend, etc.) from an investment.

22. D: Management risk refers to the impact that bad management decisions or other internal missteps can have on a company's performance and on the value of investments in that company. Market risk, or systematic risk, is the potential for loss due to the performance of the financial market. Investment risk is the risk that an investment's performance will be worse than expected. Financial risk is a generic term describing a variety of risk types, including credit risk, liquidity risk, and operational risk.

23. B: Under Regulation T, the maximum amount of the total purchase price of a stock for new purchases that a firm can lend a customer is 50%.

24. A: Firms must notify employees of their business continuity or disaster recovery plans at least annually.

25. B: A municipal bond would be the most suitable investment for an investor in a high tax bracket who wants to avoid paying any taxes on his investments. Municipal bonds are tax-exempt, so investors do not have to pay taxes on the interest from the bonds. By contrast, investors do have to pay taxes on the interest from corporate bonds, mutual funds, and preferred stocks.

26. C: Margin in a brokerage account is borrowed money that is used to purchase securities. The difference between the purchase price and the current value is called capital gains. The difference between the beginning value and the current value of an account would also be considered capital gains. Purchasing power is all available funds (unsettled, liquid, and borrowed) that can be used to purchase securities.

27. D: A UTMA account terminates when the minor reaches the age of 21.

28. A: Discretionary trading authority is when a person other than the account holder may invest without consulting the account holder about the price, amount, or type of security or the timing of the trades that are placed for the account.

29. D: A person who acts nervously or anxiously when answering questions about their objectives would raise a red flag when opening an account for a new client. It is common to find new investors who have no experience in the financial markets. While having a client with poor spending habits is unfortunate, it is not a sign of acting in bad faith. Customers can sometimes be skeptical about providing personal details, especially financial information.

30. C: Dividing a larger transaction into smaller transactions to avoid triggering a reporting or recordkeeping requirement is called structuring or smurfing. Layering is the second step in money laundering in which the criminal conceals the source of their money by executing multiple transactions. Fraud is an umbrella term for criminal activity such as tax fraud, credit card fraud, or securities fraud. Money laundering is the process of taking money that was generated from illegal activity and making it appear that it was earned legitimately.

31. D: Officers, directors, and employees are all persons that are considered to be corporate insiders.

32. A: Systematic risk, also known as market risk, affects the entire market rather than a specific security or industry. Credit risk is the risk that a lender takes on, arising from the uncertainty of whether a borrower will be able to repay what they have been loaned. Liquidity risk is the risk that an investor, firm, or institution may suffer a capital loss from having to liquidate assets at an unfavorable time (e.g., selling off assets at lower prices because funds are needed immediately). Interest rate risk is the risk of investments losing value due to changes in prevailing interest rates.

33. C: Tax risk is the risk that the state or federal governments will make unfavorable changes to tax law. Market risk is the potential for loss due to the performance of the financial market. Event risk is the risk of an unexpected event negatively affecting an investment's value. Liquidity risk is the risk that an investor, firm, or institution may suffer a capital loss from having to liquidate assets at an unfavorable time (e.g., selling off assets at lower prices because funds are needed immediately).

34. B: A stock split is a maneuver used by a company that increases the number of shares outstanding by exchanging a specified number of new shares of stock for each outstanding share. A stock dividend is a distribution made by a company to its shareholders of additional shares of stock. Stock valuation is the process of determining the value of the shares of a company's stock. When a company uses its capital to repurchase shares it has previously issued, this is called a stock buyback.

35. D: Dollar-cost averaging is the process of investing a fixed dollar amount in a security at fixed intervals.

36. C: A reverse stock split is the strategy where a company reduces the number of shares outstanding by exchanging a fractional amount of a new share for each outstanding share of stock. A stock split is a maneuver used by a company to increase the number of shares outstanding by exchanging a specified number of new shares of stock for each outstanding share. A stock dividend is a distribution made by a company to its shareholders of additional shares of stock. There is no such thing as a reverse stock dividend.

37. A: If a company declares a 1:2 reverse stock split, an investor with 200 shares will own 100 shares after the split.

38. D: Goodwill is an intangible asset that is the result of the acquisition of one company by another for a premium value. Market value is what others are willing to pay for an asset on the open market. The book value is the difference between a company's total assets and total liabilities. Acquisition value or acquisition cost is the price paid for the acquisition of an asset, including all taxes, fees, charges, and other expenses.

39. C: Preferred stocks have a prior claim on the income and assets of the issuing firm, have fixed dividends, and are issued as an alternative to debt, but do not have an effect on EPS.

40. B: American depositary receipts (ADRs) are dollar-denominated negotiable receipts for company stock of a foreign company held in trust in a foreign branch of a U.S. bank. An initial public offering (IPO) refers to the event of a company first offering its shares for sale to the public. An alternative minimum tax (AMT) is a backup tax designed to ensure that high earners cannot use tax avoidance strategies to lower their tax liability below a certain level. Automated teller machines (ATMs) are machines that can be used to deposit or withdraw funds from a customer's bank account.

41. C: The opening price of ABC Corporation should be $25.59 on December 6 ($25.34 + $0.25). Since a dividend of $0.25 per share was announced after the market closed on December 5, each share became more valuable by that amount. It's always possible for stocks to not trade at what they're supposed to, given a free market, but assuming rational market behavior, ABC stock would trade at the sum of its closing price ($25.34) plus the declared dividend amount ($0.25): $25.59.

42. D: The investor will receive 40 shares of XYZ stock on the payment date. A stock dividend is a distribution made by a company to its shareholders of additional shares of stock. Since the company is issuing each shareholder an extra $\frac{1}{5}$ share (20%) for every share owned, an individual who holds 200 shares will receive $200 \times \frac{1}{5} = 40$ new shares of XYZ Company.

43. C: An investment must be held for one year and one day to be considered long term. Anything less is considered short term.

44. C: Equity represents the amount of stockholders' capital in a firm. Assets are resources held by the company that have immediate value or that will provide a future benefit. A liability is an obligation, financial or otherwise, that the company owes to a person or business entity. Cash flow is the amount of cash moving into and out of a company.

45. C: The cash flow statement provides a summary of a company's cash flow and other events that caused changes in their cash position. The income statement reports a company's revenue over a specified time period, along with the expenses the company incurred to generate that revenue. The balance sheet is a summary report of a company's assets and liabilities, along with stockholder equity. An annual report is a document describing operations and financial position that every company listed on the stock market must provide to its shareholders.

46. C: The yield curve is the graph that represents the relationship between a bond's term to maturity and its yield at a given point in time. The efficient frontier is the upper limit of how much growth a portfolio can expect to see given its level of acceptable risk. A point-and-figure chart plots price movement without looking at time. Bar charts show multiple prices over time.

47. D: An index mutual fund is the most likely to be passively managed because it seeks to mimic the performance of a specified index by holding the same stocks as the chosen index. Bond, growth, and income funds are all actively managed by portfolio managers who pick and choose different securities depending on the type of fund and the investment goal.

48. D: A wrap account is an account in which customers with large portfolios pay a brokerage firm a flat annual fee that covers the cost of a money manager's services and the cost of commissions.

49. B: The current ratio is 3.29%.

$$\frac{\$280{,}000 \text{ (current assets)}}{\$85{,}000 \text{ (current liabilities)}} = 3.29\%$$

50. B: The book value per share is $43.42.

$$\frac{\$170{,}000 \text{ (stockholder equity)} - \$5{,}000 \text{ (preferred dividends)}}{3{,}800 \text{ (outstanding shares of common stock)}} = \$43.42$$

51. B: NASDAQ is the over-the-counter (OTC) market.

52. D: An order to sell a stock at a specific price or better is a limit order. Answers A and C are examples of a market order. Answer B is an example of a stop order.

53. A: The customer's name is not required on an order ticket. The type of order, account number, and symbol are all required items on an order ticket.

54. B: Stock trades ordinarily settle on a T+2 schedule, meaning that the settlement date is two business days following the trade date (T). Therefore, a stock trade executed on Friday, January 2, would settle on Tuesday, January 6, since weekends do not count as business days.

55. C: In TY 2023, the maximum contribution that a 45-year-old may make into a traditional IRA is $6,500.

56. B: The maximum annual contribution amount allowed in a Coverdell Education Savings Account (CESA) in TY 2023 is $2,000.

57. A: The tax consequence to an individual over the age of 59 ½ who withdraws a lump sum from his 401(k) is that the amount withdrawn is considered income and is subject to income taxes at the individual's current rate.

58. A: Capital gains and losses inside an IRA are not reported on an individual's income taxes each year.

59. C: An individual converts his $100,000 traditional IRA into a Roth IRA just before a major market decline causes the value to drop to $50,000. This investor should recharacterize the Roth IRA back to a traditional IRA to avoid paying taxes on the extra $50,000.

60. B: An option that is written against stock owned is a covered option. When a trader sells an options contract without actually owning the underlying asset, this is called a naked option. An options order is classified as buy-to-open when a trader is seeking to establish a new position (call or put) in a given option. In contrast, an options order is classified as buy-to-close when the trader is seeking to close out an existing position.

61. B: All gains and losses on options are treated as short-term gains or losses for tax purposes.

62. D: All of the statements are true. REITS are professionally managed, allow smaller investors to participate in capital appreciation and income returns of real estate without owning any property, and returns can be very volatile.

63. D: Common stockholders have the right by ownership to vote on proposed stock splits, corporate bond issuance, and the election of the corporation's board of directors.

64. B: Stockholders are allowed only one vote for every share owned. The statutory method provides for voting equal amounts of votes over more than one candidate, the cumulative method involves casting all votes for one candidate, and there are two methods for stockholder voting, statutory and cumulative.

65. B: Shareholders will retain proportionate interest in residual assets in the event of bankruptcy, may receive a list of shareholders, and may inspect a corporation's books and records. They do not have the right to access and review a corporation's confidential financial information.

66. A: A warrant is valid for a set period of time, and does not become invalid because of movement in the market price of the stock. An investor who holds a warrant may sell the warrant to another investor or exercise the warrant to purchase common stock at the subscription price.

67. C: A transfer agent does not verify company debt; this is the role of the registrar. A transfer agent does maintain the list of stockholders, verifies the correct issuance of shares, and handles the new issuance of stock certificates.

68. C: Stock market prices, permits for building, and changes in business and consumer borrowing are all considered to be leading economic indicators in that they each act as signals of an impending change to the economy and, accordingly, can be observed prior to the actual change. Corporate profits and losses are considered to be lagging economic indicators in that these types of effects are more observable after the change in the economy has already occurred.

69. C: Property, when categorized on a corporation's balance sheet, is considered a fixed asset. Other assets can include a corporation's trademarks, patents, and goodwill.

70. B: The value of a country's produced goods and services is its gross domestic product (GDP). Disintermediation involves investors moving their money from low-yielding investments to higher-yielding ones. The real GDP is a deflation- and inflation-adjusted version of the value of a country's produced goods and services. The consumer price index (CPI) is a tool utilized to measure the rise and fall of overall prices in the country by monitoring the price changes of a specific group of goods and services chosen for their high degree of use in individual lives.

71. B: The government, in moving to slow down the economy, would reduce spending and increase taxes so as to reduce overall demand for goods and services and decrease the level of money that consumers have access to.

72. D: A not-held order gives discretion to the broker as to timing and price for the order's execution. A fill-or-kill order must be executed immediately upon receipt, or it must be cancelled. An all-or-none order indicates that the investor would like all of the securities bought or sold in the transaction or none at all. A market-on-open order indicates the investor's wish to have it executed right at the opening of the market or as close to it as possible.

73. A: A buy 275 PPG at $21 stop order will allow this investor to pay no more than $21 per share in filling the short position, which has a sell price of $26 per share. A profit will still be made. Conversely, a buy 275 PPG at $32 stop order will enable their order to go as high as $32 a share before being executed, thus potentially eliminating a profit being made by this investor on the short position.

74. C: When orders come in at the same price, they are filled based on priority (first in, first executed), precedence (the larger of the orders is executed first), and parity (if all orders are the same, outstanding orders and shares are divided and shared).

75. D: Actions falling under the role of a dealer include participating in trades by trading in and out of his or her own account, such as using securities in the account to fill a buy order or buying securities for the account to fill a customer's sell order. Further, making a market in a security is also an action performed by a dealer. Conversely, a broker simply facilitates order execution for a customer, while not participating in the transaction, and charges a commission for their services.

SIE Practice Test #3

1. Which of the following are considered institutional investors?

a. A governmental entity
b. An employee benefit plan that meets the requirement of Section 403(b) or Section 457 of the Internal Revenue Code and has at least 100 participants
c. A qualified plan as defined in Section 3(a)(12)(C) of the Exchange Act and that has at least 100 participants
d. All of the above

2. What is the time-of-day restriction when placing cold calls (telemarketing)?

a. Before 8:00 a.m. and after 9:00 p.m. (local time of the caller's location)
b. Before 8:00 a.m. and after 9:00 p.m. (local time of the called party's location)
c. Before 8:00 a.m. and after 8:00 p.m. (local time of the caller's location)
d. Before 8:00 a.m. and after 8:00 p.m. (local time of the called party's location)

3. Which of the following would be considered a breakpoint sale?

a. A customer purchasing $150,000 in multiple mutual funds and paying the full sales charge of each.
b. A customer receiving a 20% discount on an equity trade.
c. A customer purchasing a municipal bond above par.
d. A customer purchasing a corporate bond below par.

4. Which of the following are prohibited activities?

a. Churning
b. Front running
c. Insider trading
d. All of the above

5. Which of the following is not a general consideration regarding communications with the public about variable life insurance and variable annuities?

a. Prospectus delivery
b. Product Identification
c. Liquidity
d. Claims about guarantees

6. Which of the following is true regarding recommendations?

a. Must have a reasonable basis
b. The market price at the time of the recommendation must be shown
c. Supporting information should be provided or offered
d. All of the above

7. When must a Form U5 be filed?

a. At the time of employment with a member firm
b. At the time of termination of employment from a member firm
c. Annually for each registered representative employed by a member firm
d. Every three years for each registered representative employed by a member firm

8. When must political contributions be disclosed to the MSRB?

a. Quarterly
b. Semiannually
c. Annually
d. Never

9. Which of the following is false regarding options-related advertisements?

a. Must be approved in advance by a Registered Options Principal
b. Copies must be retained by the member firm
c. Records containing the name of the persons who created and approved the advertisement must be kept
d. FINRA never needs to approve options-related advertisements

10. Before a registered representative may recommend the purchase or exchange of a deferred variable annuity, he or she must have a reasonable basis to believe all of the following except:

a. The transaction is suitable
b. The customer will not need the funds invested
c. The customer would benefit from certain features such as tax-deferred growth
d. The customer has been informed of various features such as a surrender period and surrender charge

11. A member may not publish a research report regarding a subject company for which the member acted as manager or co-manager of a secondary offering for _______ days following the date of the offering.

a. 10 calendar days
b. 10 business days
c. 20 calendar days
d. 20 business days

12. Which of the following must be disclosed in a research report?

a. Ownership and material conflicts of interest
b. Receipt of compensation
c. If the member was making a market in the subject company's securities at the time that research report was published
d. All of the above

13. What is the tentative prospectus circulated by the underwriters of a new of stock that is pending approval the SEC?

a. Red herring
b. IPO
c. Registration statement
d. Private placement

14. Beginning in TY 2023, what is the basic exclusion limit on tax-free transfers during life or at death (the unification of gift and estate taxes)?

a. $11,140,000
b. $11,580,000
c. $12,060,000
d. $12,920,000

15. What is the cost basis of securities given as a gift?

a. The average of the high and low prices on the date of the gift
b. The purchase price of the securities when they were originally bought
c. The average of the current market price and the price originally paid
d. None of the above

16. Which of the following is not a purpose of the Securities Act of 1933?

a. Require that investors receive financial and other significant information
b. Guarantee the financial information received by investors is accurate
c. Prohibit deceit, misrepresentations, and fraud in the sale of securities
d. Require the registration of securities

17. Which of the following is an SRO?

a. New York Stock Exchange
b. NASDAQ Stock Market
c. Chicago Board of Options
d. All of the above

18. Which of the following items should not be taken into consideration when determining investment suitability?

a. Annual income
b. Investment experience
c. Net worth
d. None of the above

19. Which of the following investments would be most appropriate for an investor with an objective of capital preservation?

a. Preferred stock
b. Certificate of deposit
c. Municipal bond
d. Corporate bond

20. What is another name for the investment objective of total return?

a. Growth
b. Income
c. Growth and income
d. Preservation of capital

21. Which of the following scenarios is the best example of diversification?

a. An investor buys 1,000 shares of ABC stock at $25 per share
b. An investor who invests $25,000 in one corporate bond
c. An investor who invests $25,000 in a large cap growth mutual fund
d. An investor who invests a total of $25,000 between stocks, bonds, and mutual funds.

22. Which of the following statements is false regarding modern portfolio theory?

a. It is a scientific approach to measuring risk.
b. It guarantees against long-term losses.
c. It involves calculating projected returns of various portfolio combinations.
d. It is the concept of minimizing risk by combining volatile and price-stable investment in a single portfolio.

23. Which of the following are examples of information security to protect customers' personal information?

a. Encrypted email
b. Password-protected laptops
c. Printing only the last four digits of Social Security numbers on documents
d. All of the above

24. Which of the following investments would be the least suitable for an elderly investor who is risk averse?

a. Municipal bond
b. Corporate bond
c. Mutual fund
d. Common stock

25. Which of the following investors would be best suited to invest in US Treasuries?

a. A 25-year-old interested in speculative investments
b. A 25-year-old with an investment objective of growth
c. A retired individual with an investment objective of growth
d. A retired individual with an investment objective of income

26. In a joint tenancy with rights of survivorship (JTWROS) account, what happens to the assets when the first person dies?

a. 50% of the assets are transferred to an estate account for the deceased person
b. 100% of the assets remain with the surviving co-account holder
c. 50% of the assets are transferred directly to the deceased person's heirs
d. 100% of the assets are transferred to an estate account for the deceased person

27. Who is/are the authorized person(s) on an estate account?

a. An attorney
b. A financial advisor
c. The heir(s)
d. The personal representative(s)

28. How long must a member firm maintain client account statements?

a. 1 year
b. 3 years
c. 6 years
d. 10 years

29. Which of the following account activities in a newly opened account would raise suspicions as a possible money laundering activity?

a. Multiple deposits that are immediately wired out of the account to a foreign bank.
b. Multiple deposits from other financial institutions that fund the purchases of several securities that remain in the account.
c. One large deposit that is only partially invested in securities.
d. Funds received via Fedwire

30. ________ is the process that criminals use to try to hide or disguise the source of their illegal money by converting it into funds that appear legitimate.

a. Layering
b. Structuring
c. Laundering
d. Blackmail

31. The practice of buying and selling stocks rapidly throughout the day in the hope that the stocks will continue climbing or falling in value for the seconds to minutes that they are owned allowing for quick profits to be made is called ___________.

a. Buy and hold
b. Active trading
c. Market timing
d. Day trading

32. Which of the following investments would not be a suitable recommendation for an IRA?

a. Common stock
b. Corporate bond
c. Municipal bond
d. Mutual fund

33. The possibility of higher prices in the future reducing the amount of goods or services that may be bought is known as ___________.

a. Market risk
b. Purchasing power risk
c. Financial risk
d. Interest rate risk

34. What is the name for stocks that have been sold and then repurchased (and held) by the issuing firm?

a. Outstanding stock
b. Treasury stock
c. Issued stock
d. Restricted stock

35. A _________ is an equity investment representing ownership in a corporation.

a. Corporate bond
b. Common stock
c. Warrant
d. Right

36. A company declares a 2:1 stock split. An investor who currently owns 100 shares of stock will have how many shares after the split?

a. 50 shares
b. 100 shares
c. 150 shares
d. 200 shares

37. Selling a security to generate a loss and then immediately buying the security back is a _______.

a. Capital loss
b. Whipsaw
c. Wash sale
d. Tax loss sale

38. Which of the following is an option issued by a given company to buy one or more shares of common stock in that company at a price initially above the market price?

a. Right
b. Warrant
c. Call
d. Put

39. The market in which securities are traded after they have been issued is the _______?

a. Primary market
b. Money market
c. Super market
d. Secondary market

40. Which of the following risks are associated with investing internationally?

a. Foreign currency risk
b. Market risk
c. Event risk
d. All of the above

41. What is the last date that ABC Corporation stock can be purchased to receive the dividend?

On November 1, ABC Corporation declared a $0.25 dividend to shareholders of record on Monday, December 5, payable on December 15.

a. December 1
b. December 5
c. December 12
d. December 15

42. A customer purchases 100 shares of ABC stock at $35/share and pays $85 in commissions. What is the cost basis?

a. $3,415
b. $3,500
c. $3,585
d. $3,600

43. _______ represents the resources of a company.

a. Assets
b. Liabilities
c. Equity
d. Cash flow

44. Which financial statement shows the company's assets, liabilities, and shareholders' equity?

a. Income statement
b. Balance sheet
c. Cash flow statement
d. Annual report

45. Municipal bonds backed by the full faith and credit, and taxing power, of the issuer are called ___________.

a. Revenue bonds
b. General obligation bonds
c. Agency bonds
d. Treasury notes

46. Which of the following statements is false regarding an upward-sloping yield curve?

a. It indicates that yields tend to increase with longer maturities.
b. The longer the time span until maturity, the greater potential for price volatility.
c. The longer the time span until maturity, the greater the risk for loss.
d. It indicates that short-term rates are higher than long-term rates.

47. What is the measure of bond price volatility that captures both price and reinvestment risks indicating how a bond will react to different interest rate environments?

a. Yield
b. Duration
c. Immunization
d. Beta

Use the following information to answer the next two questions.

Net profit after taxes:	$18,000	Stockholder's Equity:	$170,000
Total revenues:	$615,000	Preferred dividends:	$5,000
Total assets:	$340,000	Number of common shares outstanding:	3,800
Current assets:	$280,000	Current liabilities:	$85,000
Earnings per share:	$4.75	Market price:	$49.50

48. What is the return on assets (ROA)?

a. 2.92%
b. 3.29%
c. 4.76%
d. 5.29%

49. What is the return on equity (ROE)?

a. 2.92%
b. 5.29%
c. 10.42%
d. 10.59%

50. What is the term for the standard of conduct or moral judgment?

a. Values
b. Ethics
c. Conscience
d. Golden rule

51. An order to buy or sell a stock at the best available price when the order is placed is a ________ order.

a. Limit
b. Stop
c. Market
d. Stop limit

52. Which of the following is an example of a stop order?

a. An order to sell 100 shares of XYZ at the best price available
b. An order to sell 100 shares of XYZ (currently trading at $50) if the price drops to $45
c. An order to buy 100 shares of XYZ at the best price available
d. An order to buy 100 shares of XYZ at $40 or less

53. It is the responsibility of the __________ to ensure that a customer receives the correct breakpoint.

a. Registered representative
b. Customer
c. Mutual fund company
d. Broker-dealer

54. A stock trade executed on Wednesday, December 31, will settle on what date?

a. Monday, January 5
b. Tuesday, January 6
c. Wednesday, January 7
d. Thursday, January 8

55. What is the maximum amount that may be contributed to a 529 plan in TY 2023?

a. $2,000
b. $5,500
c. $6,500
d. $17,000

56. What is the tax consequence to an individual who rolls over his 401(K) directly to a traditional IRA?

a. The amount that is rolled over is considered income and is subject to income taxes at the individual's rate.
b. The amount that is rolled over is considered income and is subject to income taxes at the individual's current rate. Plus, if the individual is under age 59 ½, he may be subject to a 10% penalty.
c. If the individual is under age 59 ½, he must pay a 10% penalty. Otherwise, there are no tax consequences.
d. None of the above. A direct rollover from a 401(K) to a traditional IRA is not a taxable event.

57. An individual who withdraws a lump sum from a qualified plan can avoid income taxes and penalties if the entire amount is rolled over into a traditional IRA within _____ days.

a. 30 days
b. 45 days
c. 60 days
d. 90 days

58. By what date must an individual take his first required minimum distribution (RMD)?

a. At any time in the year he turns 70.5
b. By April 15 in the year following the year he turns 70.5
c. By December 31 in the year he turns 70.5
d. On the date that he turns 70.5

59. What is the income limit for single individuals to contribute to a Roth IRA in TY 2023?

a. $139,000
b. $144,000
c. $153,000
d. $161,000

60. The price at which you can buy a security with a call is the ________.

a. Purchase price
b. Sale price
c. Offering price
d. Strike price

61. Which of the following statements is true regarding the maximum profit and loss that the writer of an uncovered call option may realize?

a. The maximum profit is the premium amount.
b. The maximum loss is the premium amount.
c. The maximum profit is limitless.
d. The maximum loss is the strike price times the number of shares.

62. Which of the following can be defined as a *security*?

a. Fixed annuities
b. Variable annuities
c. Individual retirement accounts (IRAs)
d. All of the above

63. Which of the following are true of the term *equity*?

I. It is interchangeable with the term *stock*.
II. It provides the investor with ownership stake in the issuing corporation.
III. The shares do not mature and are therefore perpetual.
IV. A corporation's goal in selling shares is to create capital.

a. II, III, and IV
b. II only
c. I, II, III, and IV
d. I and II

64. What is stock that has been authorized for sale and sold to investors (regardless of its current ownership) considered to be?

a. Issued stock
b. Authorized stock
c. Treasury stock
d. Outstanding stock

65. Which of the following actions regarding stock PIX would be considered a violation for any registered representative?

a. Rushing a customer to purchase stock PIX specifically to qualify prior to the ex-dividend date
b. Making a customer recommendation to purchase stock PIX simply to benefit from a pending dividend payment
c. Recommending a purchase of stock PIX to a customer by highlighting the pending dividend payment as an incentive while neglecting to educate him or her on the stock's fundamentals, appropriateness, risks, and rewards
d. All of the above are violations.

66. Corporation PIX is behind on paying out a dividend on its 6% cumulative preferred stock. It has not paid a dividend for the past two years as well as the current year. What is the amount per share the owners of these shares should be paid to be current, and which of the following should be paid their dividend first: owners of cumulative preferred shares or common shareholders?

a. $12 per share, cumulative preferred shareholders
b. $18 per share, common stock shareholders
c. $180 per share, cumulative preferred shareholders
d. $18 per share, cumulative preferred shareholders

67. What would the calculated current yield be for an investor given the following information?

Investor buys 200 shares of stock PIX @ $45 per share.
Stock PIX is currently trading @ $52 per share.
Co. PIX pays a quarterly dividend of $1.25.

a. 9.6%
b. 2.8%
c. 2.4%
d. 11%

68. The Federal Reserve acts to guide and control the monetary policy of the country. Which of the following are actions it might take to do that?

a. Alter the level of money that is circulated.
b. Actively participate in open market transactions involving US government securities.
c. Publicly communicate its views regarding the economy.
d. All of the above actions will work.

69. Which of the following is a consequence of the Federal Reserve increasing the discount rate?

a. A slowing of the economy
b. Demand increases
c. Reduction in all other rates
d. None of the above

70. Of the different types of economic indicators, which type acts to provide confirmation of the state of the economy based on indicators that occur for a period of time after a change in its direction occurs?

a. Lagging indicators
b. Coincident indicators
c. Leading indicators
d. All of the above

71. What is the type of company whose earnings are easily affected and impacted by whatever the state of the overall economy is?

a. Defensive
b. Growth
c. Cyclical
d. None of the above

72. All of the following are true of market orders except that

a. they will be executed at the best possible price available.
b. they guarantee a maximum or minimum executed price for the order.
c. they can either be a buy or sell order.
d. they guarantee that the order will be executed immediately upon being introduced to the market.

73. An investor places an order to buy 250 PPG 62.15 GTC DNR. The stock closes the prior day at 63.10. Further, the stock goes ex dividend for 0.15 and accordingly will open with the market the next day at 62.95. Given these developments, which of the following depicts what the investor's buy order will be as of market opening the next day?

a. Buy 250 PPG 62.95 GTC DNR
b. Buy 250 PPG 62.15 GTC DNR
c. Buy 250 PPG 62 GTC
d. None of the above

74. What is a dealer violation involving a dealer not honoring his or her published NASDAQ quote called?

a. Backing away
b. Pulling out
c. Canceling
d. Revocation

75. What is an investment that involves investors receiving interest and principal payments on a monthly basis as a result of individual mortgages being paid down known as?

a. A pass-through
b. Separate Trading of Registered Interest and Principal of Securities (STRIP)
c. Collateralized mortgage obligation
d. TIPS

Answer Key and Explanations for Test #3

1. D: A governmental entity, an employee benefit plan that meets the requirement of Section 403(b) or Section 457 of the Internal Revenue Code and has at least 100 participants, and a qualified plan, as defined in Section 3(a)(12)(C) of the Exchange Act, that has at least 100 participants are all considered institutional investors.

2. B: The time-of-day restriction when placing cold calls is before 8:00 a.m. and after 9:00 p.m. (local time of the called party's location).

3. A: A breakpoint sale takes place when an investor invests in investment company shares at a level below where the sales charge would be reduced (the breakpoint). Equities, municipal bonds, and corporate bonds are not investment company shares.

4. D: Churning, front-running, and insider trading are all prohibited activities. Churning involves a broker, or someone trading on behalf of a customer, processing excessive transactions with the goal of increasing their commissions from trades. Front-running is an unethical, and generally illegal, activity in which a broker makes advantageous trades by using non-public information about an impending transaction. Insider trading is the illegal use of non-public information about a company by a person within that company to profit in the stock market.

5. A: Prospectus delivery is not a general consideration regarding communications with the public about variable life insurance and variable annuities. Product identification, liquidity, and claims about guarantees are general considerations.

6. D: When making recommendations, there must be a reasonable basis, the market price at the time of the recommendation must be shown, and supporting information should be provided or offered.

7. B: A Form U5 must be filed when a registered individual's employment with a member firm is terminated.

8. A: Political contributions must be reported to the MSRB by the last day of the month following the end of each calendar quarter (January 31, April 30, July 31, and October 31).

9. D: FINRA's Advertising Regulation Department *must* approve certain options communications with the public. Options-related advertisements also must be approved in advance by a Registered Options Principal, have copies retained by the member firm, and keep records containing the name of the persons who created and approved the advertisement (see FINRA Rule 2220).

10. B: A registered representative (RR) does not need to have a reasonable basis to believe that the customer will not need the funds invested before recommending the purchase or exchange of a deferred variable annuity. The RR must have a reasonable basis to believe that the transaction is suitable, that the customer would benefit from certain features such as tax-deferred growth, and that the customer has been informed of various features such as a surrender period and surrender charge.

11. A: A member may not publish a research report regarding a subject company for which the member acted as manager or co-manager of a secondary offering for 10 calendar days following the date of the offering.

12. D: Ownership and material conflicts of interest, receipt of compensation, and if the member was making a market in the subject company's securities at the time that research report was published must all be disclosed in a research report.

13. A: The tentative, or preliminary, prospectus circulated by the underwriters of a new issue of stock that is pending approval by the SEC is known as a red herring. An initial public offering (IPO) refers to the event of a company first offering its shares for sale to the public. Before shares can be offered to the public, a company must file a registration statement, or prospectus, with the SEC. A private placement is a securities transaction in which shares are sold only to a select set of entities.

14. D: Beginning in TY 2023, the basic exclusion limit on tax-free transfers during life or at death (the unification of gift and estate taxes) is $12,920,000.

15. D: The cost basis of securities given as a gift depends both (1) on whether the original cost exceeds the donation-date FMV and (2) on what the final selling price is. If the original cost is less than the donation-date FMV, then the original cost becomes the donee's basis. If the original cost exceeds the donation-date FMV, then we look to the final selling price. If the final selling price exceeds the original cost, then the original cost becomes the basis. If the final selling price is between the original cost and the donation-date FMV, then the sale price itself becomes the basis (such that no gain or loss is recognized). If the final selling price is less than the donation-date FMV, then the donation-date FMV becomes the basis. For example, a stock was purchased for $100 but valued at $80 when donated. If the donee later sells it for $110, his capital gain is $110 – $100 = $10. If the donee later sells it for $90, he has no capital gain or loss ($90 – $90). If the donee later sells it for $65, his capital loss is $80 – $65 = $15.

16. B: The Securities Act of 1933 requires that investors receive financial and other significant information and that securities be registered, but it does not guarantee the information is accurate. The act also prohibits deceit, misrepresentation, and fraud in the sale of securities.

17. D: The New York Stock Exchange, NASDAQ Stock Market, and Chicago Board Options Exchange are all self-regulatory organizations (SROs).

18. D: Annual income, investment experience, and net worth should all be taken into consideration when determining investment suitability.

19. B: A certificate of deposit would be the most appropriate investment for an investor with an objective of capital preservation. Preferred stock can lose value just like common stock, so it wouldn't be a good investment for someone who wants to retain the value of the security. Bonds would not be the best way to preserve an investment because the value of bonds, both municipal and corporate, are directly tied to interest rates, which can rise or fall depending on economic circumstances.

20. C: Growth and income is another name for the investment objective of total return. Someone with a goal of capital preservation is known as a conservative investor.

21. D: An investor who invests a total of $25,000 between stocks, bonds, and mutual funds is the best example of diversification.

22. B: The modern portfolio theory does not guarantee against long-term losses.

23. D: Encrypted email, password-protected laptops, and printing only the last four digits of Social Security numbers on documents are all examples of information security to protect customers' personal information.

24. D: A common stock would be the least suitable investment for an elderly investor who is risk averse. While municipal bonds, corporate bonds, and mutual funds can lose their value, they are statistically less volatile than common stock.

25. D: A retired individual with an investment objective of income would be the investor best suited to invest in US Treasury bonds. US Treasury bonds, or T-Bills, are best suited for older, conservative investors because they are most likely to both retain their value and generate income. T-Bills are backed by the full faith and credit of the US government.

26. B: In a joint tenant with rights of survivorship (JTWROS) account, when the first person dies 100% of the assets remain with the surviving co-account holder.

27. D: Any authorized persons on an estate account are personal representatives.

28. C: Member firms must maintain client account statements for six years.

29. A: Multiple deposits that are immediately wired out of the account to a foreign bank would raise suspicions as a possible money laundering activity. All other choices are considered normal transactions and, therefore, not suspicious activity that could be seen on money laundering.

30. C: Money laundering is the process that criminals use to hide or disguise the source of their illegal money by converting it into funds that appear legitimate. Layering is the step in the money laundering process in which the criminal executes a sequence of transactions with the same money to obscure its origin. Structuring, or smurfing, is the process of dividing a larger transaction into smaller transactions to avoid triggering a reporting or recordkeeping requirement. Blackmail is a crime in which one threatens to reveal damaging information about another unless a large sum of money is paid.

31. D: The practice of buying and selling stocks rapidly throughout the day in the hope that the stocks will continue climbing or falling in value for the seconds to minutes that they are owned, allowing for quick profits to be made, is called day trading.

32. C: A municipal bond is not a suitable investment in an IRA. Since the account is tax deferred, there is no advantage to owning an investment that is tax free. Investors are required to pay taxes on earnings from common stock, corporate bonds, and mutual fund shares, so it would be worthwhile to purchase these through a tax-advantaged account such as an IRA.

33. B: Purchasing power risk is the possibility that higher prices in the future will reduce the amount of goods or services that may be bought. Market risk is the potential for loss due to the performance of the financial market. Financial risk is a generic term describing a variety of risk types, including credit risk, liquidity risk, and operational risk. Interest rate risk is the risk of investments losing value due to changes in prevailing interest rates.

34. B: Treasury stock is the name for stocks that have been sold and then repurchased (and held) by the issuing firm. Issued stock includes all company shares that have been sold to the public. Outstanding stock includes only those issued shares that are still held by the public (i.e., have not been repurchased by the company). Restricted stock are shares that are typically issued to people within the company, such as executives or board members, as part of their compensation package. The shares are restricted in that there are limitations placed on when and how they may be traded.

35. B: Common stock is an equity investment representing ownership in a corporation. Corporate bonds give investors ownership of future cash flows, meaning companies owe investors the principal of the bonds, as well as interest, at a designated point in the future. A warrant and a right both give an investor the right but not the obligation to conduct a particular transaction.

36. D: An investor who currently owns 100 shares of stock will have 200 shares after the split.

37. C: A wash sale is defined as selling a security to generate a loss and then immediately buying the security back. It does not qualify as a capital loss (or tax loss sale) to reduce an individual's taxes.

38. B: A warrant is an option issued by a given company to buy one or more shares of common stock in that company at a price initially above the market price. A right is an option to buy one or more shares of common stock in a given company when new shares are issued, at a price initially below the market price. An option with the right to buy is known as a call option, and an option with the right to sell is known as a put option. Calls and puts are contracts made between participants in the marketplace rather than issued by a company.

39. D: The market in which securities are traded after they have been issued is the secondary market. The primary market is the market in which securities are sold by the issuers to investors. The money market is where investors trade short-term debt securities such as loans, MBSs, and bonds. The third market involves trading exchange-listed stocks through an over-the-counter (OTC) market.

40. D: Investing internationally has all of the same risks as investing in any security, including market and event risk. It also has foreign currency risk.

41. A: The last date that ABC Corporation stock can be purchased to receive the dividend is December 1. The record date is Monday, December 5, so that makes the ex-dividend date Friday, December 2. Since investors must own shares of the stock before the ex-dividend date to receive a dividend, the last day to purchase ABC Corporation stock would be Thursday, December 1.

42. C: The cost basis of 100 shares of stock purchased at $35/share with an $85 commission is $3,585:

$$100 \times 35 + 85 = 3{,}585$$

43. A: Assets represent the resources of a company. A liability is an obligation, financial or otherwise, that the company owes to a person or business entity. Equity represents the amount of stockholders' capital that has been invested in a firm. Cash flow is the amount of cash moving into and out of a company.

44. B: The balance sheet is a summary report of a company's assets and liabilities, along with stockholder equity. The income statement reports a company's revenue over a specified time period, along with the expenses the company incurred to generate that revenue. The cash flow statement provides a summary of a company's cash flow and other events that caused changes in their cash position. An annual report is a document describing operations and financial position that every company listed on the stock market must provide to its shareholders.

45. B: Municipal bonds backed by the full faith and credit, and taxing power, of the issuer are called general obligation bonds. A revenue bond is a type of municipal bond that is backed by the future income of a specific municipal project that generates revenue. Agency bonds are issued by either an agency of the US government (other than the Treasury) or a government-sponsored enterprise (GSE) and may not be fully guaranteed. Treasury notes are bonds issued by the US Treasury and are backed by the full faith and credit of the US government.

46. D: A normal, upward-sloping yield curve indicates that yields tend to increase with longer maturities. It also shows that the longer the time span until maturity, the greater potential for price volatility and risk for loss. It does not indicate that short-term rates are higher than long-term rates.

47. B: Duration is the measure of bond price volatility that captures both price and reinvestment risks, indicating how a bond will react to different interest rate environments. Yield refers to the return on investment from a security. Immunization is a strategy used to mitigate risk and minimize the negative impact of changing interest rates. Beta is a calculated quantity that describes the volatility of a security by comparing its performance to that of the rest of the market.

48. D: The return on assets (ROA) is 5.29%.

$$\frac{\$18{,}000 \text{ (net profit after taxes)}}{\$340{,}000 \text{ (total assets)}} = 0.0529 = 5.29\%$$

49. D: The return on equity (ROE) is 10.59%.

$$\frac{\$18{,}000 \text{ (net profit after taxes)}}{\$170{,}000 \text{ (stockholder equity)}} = 0.1059 = 10.59\%$$

50. B: Ethics is the standard of conduct or moral judgment. Conscience refers to a person's internal sense of right and wrong. Values are a set of moral principals that influence a person's actions. The golden rule involves treating others in the way that you would want to be treated.

51. C: A market order is an order to buy or sell at the best available price at the time the order is placed. A limit order is an order to buy at or below a specific price or to sell at or above a specific price. A stop is an order to buy or sell a stock when its market price reaches or drops below a specified price. A stop limit order is an order to buy or sell at a specific price or better once a given stop price has been hit.

52. B: An order to sell at a specific price which is below the current market price is called a stop order. Answers A and C are examples of a market order. Answer D is an example of a limit order.

53. D: The broker-dealer is responsible for ensuring that clients receive the correct breakpoint.

54. A: Stock trades ordinarily settle on a T+2 schedule, meaning that the settlement date is two business days following the trade date (T). Therefore, a stock trade executed on Wednesday, December 31, would settle on Monday, January 5, which is two business days later since January 1 is a trading holiday and weekends do not count as business days.

55. D: The maximum amount that may be contributed to a 529 plan in TY 2023 is $17,000.

56. D: The tax consequence to an individual who rolls over his 401(K) directly to a traditional IRA is nothing. A direct rollover from a 401(K) to a traditional IRA is not a taxable event.

57. C: An individual who withdraws a lump sum from a qualified plan can avoid income taxes and penalties if the entire amount is rolled over into a traditional IRA within 60 days.

58. B: An individual must take his first required minimum distribution (RMD) by April 15 in the year following the year that he or she turns 70.5

59. C: The income limit for single individuals to contribute to a Roth IRA in TY 2023 is $153,000.

60. D: The price at which you can buy a security with a call is the strike price. The purchase price is how much investors pay for a security. The market price of a security is the current price it is being traded for on a given marketplace or exchange. Offering price refers to the stock price that investment banks initially set during an IPO.

61. A: The maximum profit the writer of an uncovered call option may realize is the premium received in exchange for the contract. The maximum loss is limitless. Writers of an uncovered option receive income via premiums for writing and selling option contracts without actually owning the underlying security. Uncovered calls are considered the riskiest types of option because the value of the security may increase infinitely and the investor must buy it to meet the call, so the eventual market price will determine the magnitude of their loss.

62. B: A security must be transferable from one individual to another and exposes the owner to risk and loss. Variable annuities are securities because they are transferable and, due to their payments being varied and unpredictable, expose the owner to some financial risk and variability in returns. Fixed annuities are not securities in that they provide for fixed payments, a guarantee on the receipt of earnings and principal, and consequently, no risk to the owner. Individual retirement accounts (IRAs) are not considered securities in that they provide for regular and predictable distributions to the owners, and thus, no risk.

63. C: Equity is interchangeable with the term *stock*, provides ownership for the investor, has no maturity, and is sold in order to provide capital to the issuing corporation.

64. A: Stock that is authorized for sale and sold to investors is issued stock, regardless of whether it still remains with investors or has subsequently been repurchased by the corporation. Authorized stock is the largest number of shares that can be sold by the corporation. Treasury stock is the stock that has been sold to the public and then repurchased by the corporation. Outstanding stock is stock that has been sold to investors and still remains with investors, having not been repurchased by the issuing corporation.

65. D: A registered representative would be committing a violation by rushing a customer to make a purchase solely to meet the ex-dividend date, recommending a purchase simply to benefit from a pending dividend, or promoting a stock by highlighting the benefit of the pending dividend while neglecting to educate him or her as to the fundamentals or appropriateness this stock may have as an investment.

66. D:

$$3 \times \$6 = \$18 \text{ per share}$$

Cumulative preferred shareholders always have priority over common stock shareholders in terms of dividend payment. They must receive both the missed dividend amounts as well as the current year's before PIX can pay any dividend to its common shareholders.

67. A:

$$\text{current yield} = \frac{\text{annual income}}{\text{current market price}}$$

$$\text{current yield} = \frac{(1.25 \times 4)}{52} = 0.096 = 9.6\%$$

68. D: The Federal Reserve may alter the level of money in circulation, actively transact in US government securities in the open market, and publicly share its views on the economy and the direction it sees it taking.

69. A: If the Federal Reserve were to increase the discount rate, all other rates would go up, demand would decrease, and ultimately, the economy would be slowed.

70. A: Lagging indicators take effect after the new direction of economy takes effect, take hold for a period of time, and provide confirmation about that change. Coincident indicators are an immediate result of even slight changes in the economy. Leading indicators occur prior to the economic change and can be looked to in order to analyze the future state of the economy.

71. C: A cyclical company is sensitive to the current state of the overall economy and reflects whatever that may be during periods of both high and low performance. A company in a defensive industry is the least sensitive to the state of the overall economy. A company in a growth industry will see faster growth than whatever the current state of the overall economy is.

72. B: Market orders do NOT guarantee a maximum or minimum executed price and in fact do not guarantee any specific price at all. Market orders can either be for a buy or sell order and are guaranteed to be filled immediately upon being introduced to the market and at the best possible price available.

73. B: The investor's order will be to buy 250 PPG 62.15 GTC DNR. The buy order remains exactly the same due to the investor stipulating the order to be do not reduce (DNR), and accordingly, the order will not be reduced to reflect the distribution of dividends.

74. A: Once quotes are published over the NASDAQ workstation, they must be honored. They are considered to be firm quotes, and a dealer refusing to honor his or her firm quotes is committing a violation known as backing away.

75. A: Pass-throughs provide investors with interest and principal payment income relative to their initial investments in pools of mortgages. The payments flow through to them on a monthly basis as the individual mortgages in the pools are paid down. A Separate Trading of Registered Interest and Principal of Securities (STRIP) is an investment that provides the opportunity to purchase separately either the principal or interest payment cash flow stream of a Treasury security. Collateralized mortgage obligations (CMOs) are similar to pass-throughs except that they are separated into different maturity schedules, or tranches, each being paid in full one at a time. Treasury inflation protected securities (TIPS) are securities whose interest payments and principal amounts are influenced by the level and movement of inflation.

How to Overcome Test Anxiety

Just the thought of taking a test is enough to make most people a little nervous. A test is an important event that can have a long-term impact on your future, so it's important to take it seriously and it's natural to feel anxious about performing well. But just because anxiety is normal, that doesn't mean that it's helpful in test taking, or that you should simply accept it as part of your life. Anxiety can have a variety of effects. These effects can be mild, like making you feel slightly nervous, or severe, like blocking your ability to focus or remember even a simple detail.

If you experience test anxiety—whether severe or mild—it's important to know how to beat it. To discover this, first you need to understand what causes test anxiety.

Causes of Test Anxiety

While we often think of anxiety as an uncontrollable emotional state, it can actually be caused by simple, practical things. One of the most common causes of test anxiety is that a person does not feel adequately prepared for their test. This feeling can be the result of many different issues such as poor study habits or lack of organization, but the most common culprit is time management. Starting to study too late, failing to organize your study time to cover all of the material, or being distracted while you study will mean that you're not well prepared for the test. This may lead to cramming the night before, which will cause you to be physically and mentally exhausted for the test. Poor time management also contributes to feelings of stress, fear, and hopelessness as you realize you are not well prepared but don't know what to do about it.

Other times, test anxiety is not related to your preparation for the test but comes from unresolved fear. This may be a past failure on a test, or poor performance on tests in general. It may come from comparing yourself to others who seem to be performing better or from the stress of living up to expectations. Anxiety may be driven by fears of the future—how failure on this test would affect your educational and career goals. These fears are often completely irrational, but they can still negatively impact your test performance.

Review Video: 3 Reasons You Have Test Anxiety
Visit mometrix.com/academy and enter code: 428468

Elements of Test Anxiety

As mentioned earlier, test anxiety is considered to be an emotional state, but it has physical and mental components as well. Sometimes you may not even realize that you are suffering from test anxiety until you notice the physical symptoms. These can include trembling hands, rapid heartbeat, sweating, nausea, and tense muscles. Extreme anxiety may lead to fainting or vomiting. Obviously, any of these symptoms can have a negative impact on testing. It is important to recognize them as soon as they begin to occur so that you can address the problem before it damages your performance.

Review Video: 3 Ways to Tell You Have Test Anxiety
Visit mometrix.com/academy and enter code: 927847

The mental components of test anxiety include trouble focusing and inability to remember learned information. During a test, your mind is on high alert, which can help you recall information and stay focused for an extended period of time. However, anxiety interferes with your mind's natural processes, causing you to blank out, even on the questions you know well. The strain of testing during anxiety makes it difficult to stay focused, especially on a test that may take several hours. Extreme anxiety can take a huge mental toll, making it difficult not only to recall test information but even to understand the test questions or pull your thoughts together.

Review Video: How Test Anxiety Affects Memory
Visit mometrix.com/academy and enter code: 609003

Effects of Test Anxiety

Test anxiety is like a disease—if left untreated, it will get progressively worse. Anxiety leads to poor performance, and this reinforces the feelings of fear and failure, which in turn lead to poor performances on subsequent tests. It can grow from a mild nervousness to a crippling condition. If allowed to progress, test anxiety can have a big impact on your schooling, and consequently on your future.

Test anxiety can spread to other parts of your life. Anxiety on tests can become anxiety in any stressful situation, and blanking on a test can turn into panicking in a job situation. But fortunately, you don't have to let anxiety rule your testing and determine your grades. There are a number of relatively simple steps you can take to move past anxiety and function normally on a test and in the rest of life.

Review Video: How Test Anxiety Impacts Your Grades
Visit mometrix.com/academy and enter code: 939819

Physical Steps for Beating Test Anxiety

While test anxiety is a serious problem, the good news is that it can be overcome. It doesn't have to control your ability to think and remember information. While it may take time, you can begin taking steps today to beat anxiety.

Just as your first hint that you may be struggling with anxiety comes from the physical symptoms, the first step to treating it is also physical. Rest is crucial for having a clear, strong mind. If you are tired, it is much easier to give in to anxiety. But if you establish good sleep habits, your body and mind will be ready to perform optimally, without the strain of exhaustion. Additionally, sleeping well helps you to retain information better, so you're more likely to recall the answers when you see the test questions.

Getting good sleep means more than going to bed on time. It's important to allow your brain time to relax. Take study breaks from time to time so it doesn't get overworked, and don't study right before bed. Take time to rest your mind before trying to rest your body, or you may find it difficult to fall asleep.

Review Video: The Importance of Sleep for Your Brain
Visit mometrix.com/academy and enter code: 319338

Along with sleep, other aspects of physical health are important in preparing for a test. Good nutrition is vital for good brain function. Sugary foods and drinks may give a burst of energy but this burst is followed by a crash, both physically and emotionally. Instead, fuel your body with protein and vitamin-rich foods.

Also, drink plenty of water. Dehydration can lead to headaches and exhaustion, especially if your brain is already under stress from the rigors of the test. Particularly if your test is a long one, drink water during the breaks. And if possible, take an energy-boosting snack to eat between sections.

Review Video: How Diet Can Affect your Mood
Visit mometrix.com/academy and enter code: 624317

Along with sleep and diet, a third important part of physical health is exercise. Maintaining a steady workout schedule is helpful, but even taking 5-minute study breaks to walk can help get your blood pumping faster and clear your head. Exercise also releases endorphins, which contribute to a positive feeling and can help combat test anxiety.

When you nurture your physical health, you are also contributing to your mental health. If your body is healthy, your mind is much more likely to be healthy as well. So take time to rest, nourish your body with healthy food and water, and get moving as much as possible. Taking these physical steps will make you stronger and more able to take the mental steps necessary to overcome test anxiety.

Mental Steps for Beating Test Anxiety

Working on the mental side of test anxiety can be more challenging, but as with the physical side, there are clear steps you can take to overcome it. As mentioned earlier, test anxiety often stems from lack of preparation, so the obvious solution is to prepare for the test. Effective studying may be the most important weapon you have for beating test anxiety, but you can and should employ several other mental tools to combat fear.

First, boost your confidence by reminding yourself of past success—tests or projects that you aced. If you're putting as much effort into preparing for this test as you did for those, there's no reason you should expect to fail here. Work hard to prepare; then trust your preparation.

Second, surround yourself with encouraging people. It can be helpful to find a study group, but be sure that the people you're around will encourage a positive attitude. If you spend time with others who are anxious or cynical, this will only contribute to your own anxiety. Look for others who are motivated to study hard from a desire to succeed, not from a fear of failure.

Third, reward yourself. A test is physically and mentally tiring, even without anxiety, and it can be helpful to have something to look forward to. Plan an activity following the test, regardless of the outcome, such as going to a movie or getting ice cream.

When you are taking the test, if you find yourself beginning to feel anxious, remind yourself that you know the material. Visualize successfully completing the test. Then take a few deep, relaxing breaths and return to it. Work through the questions carefully but with confidence, knowing that you are capable of succeeding.

Developing a healthy mental approach to test taking will also aid in other areas of life. Test anxiety affects more than just the actual test—it can be damaging to your mental health and even contribute to depression. It's important to beat test anxiety before it becomes a problem for more than testing.

Review Video: Test Anxiety and Depression
Visit mometrix.com/academy and enter code: 904704

Study Strategy

Being prepared for the test is necessary to combat anxiety, but what does being prepared look like? You may study for hours on end and still not feel prepared. What you need is a strategy for test prep. The next few pages outline our recommended steps to help you plan out and conquer the challenge of preparation.

Step 1: Scope Out the Test

Learn everything you can about the format (multiple choice, essay, etc.) and what will be on the test. Gather any study materials, course outlines, or sample exams that may be available. Not only will this help you to prepare, but knowing what to expect can help to alleviate test anxiety.

Step 2: Map Out the Material

Look through the textbook or study guide and make note of how many chapters or sections it has. Then divide these over the time you have. For example, if a book has 15 chapters and you have five days to study, you need to cover three chapters each day. Even better, if you have the time, leave an extra day at the end for overall review after you have gone through the material in depth.

If time is limited, you may need to prioritize the material. Look through it and make note of which sections you think you already have a good grasp on, and which need review. While you are studying, skim quickly through the familiar sections and take more time on the challenging parts. Write out your plan so you don't get lost as you go. Having a written plan also helps you feel more in control of the study, so anxiety is less likely to arise from feeling overwhelmed at the amount to cover.

Step 3: Gather Your Tools

Decide what study method works best for you. Do you prefer to highlight in the book as you study and then go back over the highlighted portions? Or do you type out notes of the important information? Or is it helpful to make flashcards that you can carry with you? Assemble the pens, index cards, highlighters, post-it notes, and any other materials you may need so you won't be distracted by getting up to find things while you study.

If you're having a hard time retaining the information or organizing your notes, experiment with different methods. For example, try color-coding by subject with colored pens, highlighters, or post-it notes. If you learn better by hearing, try recording yourself reading your notes so you can listen while in the car, working out, or simply sitting at your desk. Ask a friend to quiz you from your flashcards, or try teaching someone the material to solidify it in your mind.

Step 4: Create Your Environment

It's important to avoid distractions while you study. This includes both the obvious distractions like visitors and the subtle distractions like an uncomfortable chair (or a too-comfortable couch that makes you want to fall asleep). Set up the best study environment possible: good lighting and a comfortable work area. If background music helps you focus, you may want to turn it on, but otherwise keep the room quiet. If you are using a computer to take notes, be sure you don't have any other windows open, especially applications like social media, games, or anything else that could distract you. Silence your phone and turn off notifications. Be sure to keep water close by so you stay hydrated while you study (but avoid unhealthy drinks and snacks).

Also, take into account the best time of day to study. Are you freshest first thing in the morning? Try to set aside some time then to work through the material. Is your mind clearer in the afternoon or evening? Schedule your study session then. Another method is to study at the same time of day that you will take the test, so that your brain gets used to working on the material at that time and will be ready to focus at test time.

Step 5: Study!

Once you have done all the study preparation, it's time to settle into the actual studying. Sit down, take a few moments to settle your mind so you can focus, and begin to follow your study plan. Don't give in to distractions or let yourself procrastinate. This is your time to prepare so you'll be ready to fearlessly approach the test. Make the most of the time and stay focused.

Of course, you don't want to burn out. If you study too long you may find that you're not retaining the information very well. Take regular study breaks. For example, taking five minutes out of every hour to walk briskly, breathing deeply and swinging your arms, can help your mind stay fresh.

As you get to the end of each chapter or section, it's a good idea to do a quick review. Remind yourself of what you learned and work on any difficult parts. When you feel that you've mastered the material, move on to the next part. At the end of your study session, briefly skim through your notes again.

But while review is helpful, cramming last minute is NOT. If at all possible, work ahead so that you won't need to fit all your study into the last day. Cramming overloads your brain with more information than it can process and retain, and your tired mind may struggle to recall even previously learned information when it is overwhelmed with last-minute study. Also, the urgent nature of cramming and the stress placed on your brain contribute to anxiety. You'll be more likely to go to the test feeling unprepared and having trouble thinking clearly.

So don't cram, and don't stay up late before the test, even just to review your notes at a leisurely pace. Your brain needs rest more than it needs to go over the information again. In fact, plan to finish your studies by noon or early afternoon the day before the test. Give your brain the rest of the day to relax or focus on other things, and get a good night's sleep. Then you will be fresh for the test and better able to recall what you've studied.

Step 6: Take a practice test

Many courses offer sample tests, either online or in the study materials. This is an excellent resource to check whether you have mastered the material, as well as to prepare for the test format and environment.

Check the test format ahead of time: the number of questions, the type (multiple choice, free response, etc.), and the time limit. Then create a plan for working through them. For example, if you have 30 minutes to take a 60-question test, your limit is 30 seconds per question. Spend less time on the questions you know well so that you can take more time on the difficult ones.

If you have time to take several practice tests, take the first one open book, with no time limit. Work through the questions at your own pace and make sure you fully understand them. Gradually work up to taking a test under test conditions: sit at a desk with all study materials put away and set a timer. Pace yourself to make sure you finish the test with time to spare and go back to check your answers if you have time.

After each test, check your answers. On the questions you missed, be sure you understand why you missed them. Did you misread the question (tests can use tricky wording)? Did you forget the information? Or was it something you hadn't learned? Go back and study any shaky areas that the practice tests reveal.

Taking these tests not only helps with your grade, but also aids in combating test anxiety. If you're already used to the test conditions, you're less likely to worry about it, and working through tests until you're scoring well gives you a confidence boost. Go through the practice tests until you feel comfortable, and then you can go into the test knowing that you're ready for it.

Test Tips

On test day, you should be confident, knowing that you've prepared well and are ready to answer the questions. But aside from preparation, there are several test day strategies you can employ to maximize your performance.

First, as stated before, get a good night's sleep the night before the test (and for several nights before that, if possible). Go into the test with a fresh, alert mind rather than staying up late to study.

Try not to change too much about your normal routine on the day of the test. It's important to eat a nutritious breakfast, but if you normally don't eat breakfast at all, consider eating just a protein bar. If you're a coffee drinker, go ahead and have your normal coffee. Just make sure you time it so that the caffeine doesn't wear off right in the middle of your test. Avoid sugary beverages, and drink enough water to stay hydrated but not so much that you need a restroom break 10 minutes into the test. If your test isn't first thing in the morning, consider going for a walk or doing a light workout before the test to get your blood flowing.

Allow yourself enough time to get ready, and leave for the test with plenty of time to spare so you won't have the anxiety of scrambling to arrive in time. Another reason to be early is to select a good seat. It's helpful to sit away from doors and windows, which can be distracting. Find a good seat, get out your supplies, and settle your mind before the test begins.

When the test begins, start by going over the instructions carefully, even if you already know what to expect. Make sure you avoid any careless mistakes by following the directions.

Then begin working through the questions, pacing yourself as you've practiced. If you're not sure on an answer, don't spend too much time on it, and don't let it shake your confidence. Either skip it and come back later, or eliminate as many wrong answers as possible and guess among the remaining ones. Don't dwell on these questions as you continue—put them out of your mind and focus on what lies ahead.

Be sure to read all of the answer choices, even if you're sure the first one is the right answer. Sometimes you'll find a better one if you keep reading. But don't second-guess yourself if you do immediately know the answer. Your gut instinct is usually right. Don't let test anxiety rob you of the information you know.

If you have time at the end of the test (and if the test format allows), go back and review your answers. Be cautious about changing any, since your first instinct tends to be correct, but make sure you didn't misread any of the questions or accidentally mark the wrong answer choice. Look over any you skipped and make an educated guess.

At the end, leave the test feeling confident. You've done your best, so don't waste time worrying about your performance or wishing you could change anything. Instead, celebrate the successful completion of this test. And finally, use this test to learn how to deal with anxiety even better next time.

Review Video: 5 Tips to Beat Test Anxiety
Visit mometrix.com/academy and enter code: 570656

Important Qualification

Not all anxiety is created equal. If your test anxiety is causing major issues in your life beyond the classroom or testing center, or if you are experiencing troubling physical symptoms related to your anxiety, it may be a sign of a serious physiological or psychological condition. If this sounds like your situation, we strongly encourage you to seek professional help.

Tell Us Your Story

We at Mometrix would like to extend our heartfelt thanks to you for letting us be a part of your journey. It is an honor to serve people from all walks of life, people like you, who are committed to building the best future they can for themselves.

We know that each person's situation is unique. But we also know that, whether you are a young student or a mother of four, you care about working to make your own life and the lives of those around you better.

That's why we want to hear your story.

We want to know why you're taking this test. We want to know about the trials you've gone through to get here. And we want to know about the successes you've experienced after taking and passing your test.

In addition to your story, which can be an inspiration both to us and to others, we value your feedback. We want to know both what you loved about our book and what you think we can improve on.

The team at Mometrix would be absolutely thrilled to hear from you! So please, send us an email at tellusyourstory@mometrix.com or visit us at mometrix.com/tellusyourstory.php and let's stay in touch.

Additional Bonus Material

Due to our efforts to try to keep this book to a manageable length, we've created a link that will give you access to all of your additional bonus material:

mometrix.com/bonus948/seriessie